Walking the Talk

south essex college

FURTHER & HIGHER EDUCATION
SOUTHEND CAMPUS

Related titles of interest:

Delivering Effective Behaviour Support in Schools: A Practical Guide
Giles Barrow
1-85346-796-0

Improving Behaviour and Raising Self-Esteem in the Classroom: A Practical Guide to Using Transactional Analysis
Giles Barrow, Emma Bradshaw and Trudi Newton
1-85346-775-8

The Emotional Literacy Handbook: Promoting Whole-School Strategies
Antidote
1-84312-060-7

Nurturing Emotional Literacy: A Practical Guide for Teachers, Parents and those in the Caring Professions
Peter Sharp
1-85346-678-6

Walking the Talk

How transactional analysis is improving behaviour and raising self-esteem

Edited by

GILES BARROW

and

TRUDI NEWTON

 **David Fulton** Publishers

David Fulton Publishers Ltd
The Chiswick Centre, 414 Chiswick High Road, London W4 5TF

www.fultonpublishers.co.uk

First published in Great Britain in 2004 by David Fulton Publishers

10 9 8 7 6 5 4 3 2 1

David Fulton Publishers is a division of Granada Learning, part of ITV plc.

Note: The right of individual contributors to be identified as the authors of their work has been asserted by them in accordance with the Copyright, Designs and Patents Act 1988.

Copyright © Giles Barrow and Trudi Newton 2004

British Library Cataloguing in Publication Data
A catalogue record for this book is available from the British Library.

ISBN 1 84312 185 9

Designed and typeset by Kenneth Burnley, Wirral, Cheshire
Printed and bound in Great Britain

Contents

Acknowledgements

Writing and editing this book has been to experience being part of a creative and co-operative team. All the contributors have done much more than write their chapters – we have supported, challenged, negotiated, discussed and made decisions together. From our original idea of jointly writing an article as a group of educational TA practitioners, we have shared the growth of that idea to produce *Walking the Talk*. Thanks go to the staff of David Fulton Publishers, especially Linda Evans and Anne Summers, for trust, encouragement and helpful advice in that process.

Thanks also to Mary Cox, Chris Davidson and Jerome White for allowing us to use their diagrams, each of which has been important in clarifying our thinking by making ideas visible. Colleagues have permitted us to include stories that they have shared with us in training courses and workshops – thanks to all of you, and special thanks to Nicky Rosewell and the staff and children of Grange Middle School, Harrow, who have tried out many of the ideas and evaluated them for us.

Sharing TA concepts means drawing diagrams – many thanks to David Newton for doing this for us, and to Rosie Barrow and Jacob Wye for their stories and illustrations.

And, as always, thanks to everyone who has listened, reflected, questioned, teased out implications and taken TA into schools and classrooms far and wide.

Introduction

Welcome to our book. We are really pleased you decided to take some time to find out about our work and ideas. For those readers who want to start to learn immediately about what we have been developing it might be best to skip the following paragraphs and turn straight to the contents matrix on p. xiii. For those who want to know a little more about the context of this book and its contributors, read on.

IMPROVING BEHAVIOUR AND RAISING SELF-ESTEEM

An important point to make at the outset is that this is the second book that we have written describing how transactional analysis (TA) is used in education. The earlier book is *Improving Behaviour and Raising Self-Esteem* (2001) (also published by David Fulton). While it is not necessary to have read the first book in order to make sense of this one, they are very much companion titles. In our first book we demonstrated how TA concepts can be explained within the context of schools and classrooms. We described how core ideas are used to make sense of the relational aspects of teaching and learning. We provided illustrative case study material and resources to encourage practitioners to make their own paths into using TA in education.

Since its publication we have come across numerous stories of how teachers, support staff and other professionals have applied TA in their work with children and young people. We have been struck by the accounts of perseverance, creativity and resourcefulness demonstrated by both adults and youngsters in overcoming difficulties and in promoting growth and development. What we also noticed is that there has been an increasing number of professionals who now utilise TA as a key component in how they understand and shape their work with colleagues and students.

One of the recurring themes in the feedback we pick up is a growing curiosity about the core principles that underpin TA, the first of which is that anyone can learn, change and grow. This is linked to a second belief – that everyone has the capacity to think, that we can make sense of information, consider options and make decisions. The third belief is that we think most effectively when we have a sense that we are OK and that others are too:

- **I'm OK – You're OK**
- **Everyone can think**
- **Anyone can change**

This most essential aspect of TA has generated a range of discussions about what happens in classrooms and staffrooms, and a number of teachers have also discovered the statements can make for a striking wall display.

WALKING THE TALK

This second title is designed to encourage practitioners already using TA to advance their understanding and application of concepts. For those new to TA we invite you to use this book to find out about an interesting and alternative approach to the role of the educator and the learning process.

The way in which this book differs from the first is that there is a significant emphasis on describing the *application* of TA ideas, as opposed to explaining theory. All of the contributors are drawing their stories from direct and recent work with children and staff. The contributors are all practitioners in the learning process, either with adults and/or children, and their accounts combine insights about TA concepts with 'live' situations which will be familiar to many working in education. In all cases the authors are describing how they 'walk the talk' in terms of applying TA.

There are many books that draw on the experience of contributing practitioners but what might be different about this title is the process by which it has been produced. Although individual contributors have been responsible for drafting particular sections, there has been an intentional aim of collaborative contribution over each chapter. In other words, each contributor has been encouraged to comment, amend and feedback on each chapter and the overall structure of the book. Given that one of the common beliefs among the contributors is that diversity and collaboration lead to strength and potency, the process through which the book has emerged has also demonstrated 'walking the talk'.

THE BOOK IN CONTEXT

Since the publication of *Improving Behaviour and Raising Self-Esteem* in 2001, there has been a plethora of new national and regional initiatives, programmes and guidance relating to the work of educators. The DfES Behaviour Improvement Programme has expanded to include the themes of attendance and multi-professional practice across many areas of the country. Similarly, the Department's Key Stage 3 and Primary strategies have both generated a growth in interest and activities focusing on the relational aspects of the classroom. Cross-departmental programmes such as the national Children's Fund Programme and the embedding of Sure Start, in addition to the potential impact of the *Every Child Matters* (HMSO

2003) guidance, have also amplified the importance of early and multiple levels of intervention to support learning relationships outside of the formal context of the school. More generally, the growing interest in emotional literacy, thinking skills, accelerated learning and multiple intelligences indicates a shift away from the more segregated notions of teaching, learning and behaviour that permeated the 1990s.

We provide accounts about how practitioners are utilising TA concepts within the current cultural and legislative context. The stories are not about individuals surviving, overwhelmed by contending pressures and demands; instead these are stories of how individuals are discovering ways of thriving by drawing on strategies based on respect and integrity for learners, educators and organisations. These are essentially stories of our time, our children and our schools.

THE CONTRIBUTORS

The contributor team mainly comprises the members of the Sutton TA training group who have been working together for nearly three years (at time of writing). Some of the members have worked together for several more years in developing effective support for children, teachers and schools. In addition, the contributory team include the majority of UK transactional analysts currently qualified to work in the education field.

We open with a chapter by Linda Hellaby who has spent her entire career working in inner-city primary schools in the north of England. In her role as deputy head teacher she was one of the early pioneers in teaching TA directly to children. Her chapter presents a wide range of strategies for using core concepts in the classroom, both as a means for understanding and responding to children and also as tools for pupils to make sense of and manage their own lives. Complementing Linda's story is a secondary-based account provided by Pete Shotton. Initially specialising in supporting children with specific learning needs, Pete has been developing a highly successful and well-regarded learning mentoring team during the last four years. Based in a boys' comprehensive school in central Manchester, Pete describes how his team has made an impact on the experience of individual students as well as on the wider culture of the school. Both accounts capture the dynamic of working directly with youngsters and applying TA thinking and action within the context of mainstream education.

The next section focuses on the work of the Sutton LEA Behaviour Support Service. Situated in south London, the service has developed an important and successful model of support to both local secondary and primary schools. The service is highly committed to using TA and the whole team is trained to at least an introductory level in the approach, with most members undertaking advanced training and supervision. One of the central concepts that informs the work of the service is the Cycle of Development model. Team members Gill Wong, Patricia Blake and Team Leader Emma Bradshaw present vivid accounts of the impact of the model and the developmental affirmations on children and adults. Anthea

Harding, who works both independently and as part of the Sutton team, gives a description of the close case working of the individual tutor. She demonstrates a combination of TA concepts and strategies that illustrate both an effective and affective process for children and young people. A final contribution from Sutton is an exploration of how imago theory can be used to inform people how to run groups in schools. Emma Bradshaw and Gill Wong unpick the process of imago development and narrate how this applies to individual intervention in a class setting.

Ben Wye is a behaviour support teacher working for Westminster LEA. As part of his role he designed and developed a community based project aimed at preparing children for transition to secondary school. His chapter takes a detailed look at how TA ideas can provide a practical approach to addressing the potential of bullying during transition. Once again, his account is drawn directly from teaching TA with groups of children.

While most of the chapters cover work that centres on applying and teaching TA with children, final contributions from Giles Barrow and Trudi Newton reflect their work with school staff and members of support and advisory services. Giles Barrow is a teacher and works as a transactional analyst in the field of education. He works with groups of professionals, parents and children, introducing TA ideas to increase awareness and understanding about relationships. In his chapter he offers some thoughts for colleagues working in management roles in schools and considers combining solution-focused techniques with game theory. Trudi Newton is an adult educator and teaching and supervising transactional analyst who has shared TA ideas with all the contributors to this book over several years, through workshops, professional development groups, supervision and consultancy. In her chapter she explores some connections between educational philosophy and new developments in TA.

IDEAS FOR USING THIS BOOK

We anticipate that there may be different readerships for this book including professionals already using TA in their work, newcomers to TA and readers seeking ideas to improve behaviour and raise self-esteem in their classroom or school. Consequently, we have presented the content of the chapters in a way which we hope you find useful for locating what you want from the book, and this is presented in the matrix opposite.

Finally, a note on case study material. In all cases contributors have changed the names and other factors that might identify children, teachers or schools.

Chapter	Key TA concepts	Context	Theme
Teaching TA in the Primary School Linda Hellaby	Rackets; egostates; strokes	Mainstream primary classroom	Teaching TA to pupils
Saying Hello: Establishing a Pastoral Mentoring Service in an Inner-city Secondary School Pete Shotton	Cultural script; injunctions/permissions; transactions	Mainstream secondary	Mentoring
It Doesn't Matter What Age You Are – It's What Stage You Are At That Counts Gill Wong and Emma Bradshaw	Cycle of Development	Primary and secondary behaviour support	Emotional development
Keep Taking the TA: A Letter to Henri Matisse Patricia Blake	Cycle of Development	Primary behaviour support	Emotional development
Have I Got the Right Hat On? Using TA to Deliver High-quality Individual Tuition Anthea Harding	Cycle of Development; drivers, egostates, transactions	Individual tuition across primary and secondary phase	Therapeutic education
Am I In or Out? Using Imago Theory in Developing Effective Group Work Emma Bradshaw and Gill Wong	Imago theory	Primary behaviour support	Group work process
It's a Zoo Out There! Helping Children Cope with Bullying by Understanding Drivers and Permissions Ben Wye	Driver behaviour; Cycle of Development; injunctions/permissions	Transition; primary behaviour support	Transition; anti-bullying
Taking the Drama Out of a Crisis: How School Managers Use Game Theory to Promote Autonomy Giles Barrow	Drama/Winner's Triangles; game theory; autonomy	Management teams in both primary and secondary phases	Effective management of colleagues
3-D OK-ness for Schools: Developing Positive School Cultures through Three-dimensional Acceptance Trudi Newton	Life positions; cultural script; autonomy	Leadership – primary and seconday phases	Educational TA; learning process

TA Terminology

Most of the material in the following chapters draws on transactional analysis ideas introduced in *Improving Behaviour and Raising Self-Esteem in the Classroom* (Barrow *et al.* 2001). Some of the ideas have been extended further, and some new concepts have been introduced. In the following summary we define the terms that are used in the rest of this book, and indicate where their application is described in the various chapters, and where the theory is discussed in *Improving Behaviour*. The matrix on page xii shows the TA concepts included in each chapter and their application in schools. Below, the ideas presented in *Improving Behaviour* form the paragraph headings, and related ideas are grouped under each heading. All TA and other key terms are italicised.

PRINCIPLES OF TA

The philosophy and values of TA are demonstrated in the three statements in the Introduction. These are the foundation of TA thinking, and the starting point for the way the whole range of concepts and tools are developed and used. This intrinsic valuing of each individual's unique self, and of the personal resources they already have, underpins all the practice described in the following chapters.

EGOSTATES

The egostate model is the fundamental building block of TA theory. An egostate is defined as 'a consistent pattern of feeling and experience and a corresponding consistent pattern of behaviour' (Berne 1964). It is sometimes referred to as PAC (for Parent, Adult, Child). A full description of the model can be found in Barrow *et al.* 2001: 13–16.

In Chapter 1 Linda Hellaby describes how she teaches PAC to pupils. She explains both the *structural egostates* (how the content of Parent, Adult and Child, derived from our experience, comprise our personality) and the *functional* model – the different ways in which we behave when we interact with other people. The latter relates to the 'behaviour' part of Berne's definition; we use the term *behavioural modes* (Temple 1999) to show the positive and negative behaviours associated with each way of functioning (see Barrow *et al.* 2001: 16 for a chart of the characteristics of the modes). Anthea Harding, in Chapter 5, neatly shows how egostates and behaviours are linked. She describes how she uses her integrating Adult to choose an appropriate way of interacting with pupils in order to invite effective communication and behavioural change. *Integrating Adult* refers to the dynamic role of the Adult in using here-and-now awareness and reality checking to decide which behavioural mode is most likely to be successful in practice, for instance in promoting conflict resolution.

A very different situation is depicted in the *symbiosis* model, also in Chapter 5. In symbiosis it seems as if two people together use only three of the possible six egostates, i.e. as if they constituted a single person (Schiff *et al.* 1975). The other egostates are *discounted* – minimised or ignored in some way.

TRANSACTIONS

A *transaction* is an interaction consisting of a stimulus and a response. Transactions may be *complementary, crossed* or *ulterior* (Barrow *et al.* 2001: 17–19) and can be from and to any egostate. In Chapter 5 Harding introduces a constructive development known as a *bull's-eye transaction* (Woolams and Brown 1978). This comes from one person's Adult and is directed to another person's Parent (acknowledging their values and attitude), Child (recognising the driving emotion) and Adult (supporting the other's thinking).

In Chapter 2 Pete Shotton takes a model from White and White (1975) that includes nine types of transaction, between various egostates, including the 'early' egostates within the Child, called *P1, A1* and *C1* (the *second order egostate model*).

DRAMA TRIANGLE

This is a way of describing and analysing psychological games, with three roles – *Persecutor, Rescuer* and *Victim* (Karpman 1968). The Winner's Triangle (Choy 1990 and others) is a positive version, derived from the 'well-intentioned' aspect of the Drama Triangle. As tools for dealing with conflict, the triangles are explained in Chapter 8, where Giles Barrow describes using *solution-focused techniques* to facilitate the move from Drama to Winner's Triangle. Solution-focused thinking is a 'means of helping people find ways to create the life they want' (Ajmal and Rees 2001) and 'looks for solution patterns as a basis for rekindling hope and facilitating change' (Rhodes and Ajmal 1995). Giles Barrow illustrates how using TA and solution-focused concepts together can improve relationships between colleagues.

Sometimes we stop short of playing games and engage in *rackets* (English 1971). These are inauthentic and manipulative ways of behaving, feeling and thinking. In Chapter 1, Linda Hellaby explores this idea in detail as she facilitates children in identifying and expressing their real, authentic feelings.

STROKES

A *stroke* is a unit of human recognition. We all need to know that other people are aware of us, preferably by them giving us positive strokes of acceptance and approval. If we don't get enough of these we will invite negative strokes of disapproval or rejection. As Hellaby shows, in Chapter 1, strokes are of paramount importance in promoting healthy development. Unconditional positive strokes are sometimes called *warm fuzzies* (and unconditional negative strokes are *cold pricklies*).

LIFE POSITIONS (WINDOWS ON THE WORLD)

Fundamental to TA is the idea of *OK-ness*; 'I'm OK, you're OK' is a phrase well known even to people who know little about TA. This refers to one of four possible *life-positions* (Berne 1962) or ways of seeing the world as if through different windows (Hay 1996). The others are: 'I'm OK, you're not OK'; 'I'm not OK, you're OK'; and 'I'm not OK, you're not OK'.

As Trudi Newton explains, in Chapter 9, the development of this idea into *three-dimensional OK-ness* (Davidson 1999) provides a healthy model for considering change in school culture.

LIFE-SCRIPT

Our *script*, or *life-script*, is the set of decisions and beliefs that we arrived at in childhood about ourselves, others, and our place in the world. An important influence on the development of our personal script is the culture in which we grow up. The *cultural script* is carried in our Parent egostate, affecting our values, beliefs and attitudes (sometimes without our being aware of it) and also how we act, think and feel in unfamiliar situations. It is determined by our nationality, ethnic group, social class, family circumstances and gender. We can also say (as a metaphor) that organisations and groups have a cultural script. In Chapter 2, Pete Shotton uses this idea to explore and analyse the process of bringing about significant change in a school whose recent history had reinforced some negative beliefs and patterns of behaviour.

DRIVERS

Driver messages form part of the script, offering us a kind of 'conditional OK-ness' if we comply with them. Under stress we 'hear' the message and go into *driver behaviour*, often simply known as *drivers*. Ben Wye, in Chapter 7, describes the drivers in detail and shows how giving children appropriate *permissions*, or '*allowers*' can enable them to move out of their unhelpful driver behaviour and become more autonomous in stressful situations.

Each driver is associated with a preferred order of thinking, feeling and doing. These are known as *doors to contact*. For any individual, the most effective way to approach them is by their 'contact door' or 'open door', which may be any of the three (Ware 1983). In Chapter 5, Harding describes using this technique to enhance her contact with pupils. More about the theory of drivers can be found in Barrow *et al.* 2001: 109, 112–18.

CYCLES OF DEVELOPMENT

The *Cycle of Development* model was originated by Pamela Levin (1982). It describes stages in the development of children, from birth to 19 years, which are then recycled throughout life. Jean Illsley Clarke developed the educational potential of the model for parent educators (Clarke and Dawson 1998). We made further adaptations to her work to make it suitable for school use. The *stages of development* and associated *affirmations* from Barrow are reprinted in full in Appendix 1, with the addition of three new 'stages'. For a detailed explanation of the model and some school applications see Barrow *et al.* 2001: 73–82.

This model has become a core 'thinking framework' for all the contributors to this book. Chapters 3, 4 and 5 demonstrate key ways in which it informs the thinking of the Sutton Behaviour Support team and include moving case studies showing how effective this can be for diagnosis and intervention.

CONTRACTS

In TA practice, contracts are multilateral, negotiated agreements between all involved parties to bring about a mutually determined beneficial outcome. Although contracts do not feature as the main tool in any of the chapters, they are fundamental to the practice of every contributor (see Barrow *et al.* 2001, chapters 1, 3).

IMAGOS

A person's *group imago* (Berne 1963) is a mental picture of what a group is, or should be, based on previous experiences of groups, including our primary group, the family. In Chapter 6, Emma Bradshaw and Gill Wong describe stages in the development of one boy's imago through a sensitive piece of group work. In Chapter 9, Trudi Newton describes a further development of this idea to illustrate different views of educational philosophy and practice.

1

Teaching TA in the Primary School

LINDA HELLABY

INTRODUCTION

As every teacher knows, in order to learn successfully children must feel happy and secure within the school environment. In addition, they must be able to behave appropriately, communicate effectively, have self-awareness and the ability to problem-solve and resolve conflict, and also begin to learn how to protect themselves. This is in addition to the more obvious tasks of academic work.

When appointed to a new position 20 years ago, in an inner-city school in an area of severe deprivation, I soon found my class quickly disintegrated into total anarchy despite my trying all the 'correct' educational approaches. In desperation I decided to teach the children about *strokes* as I reasoned it might make them feel better about themselves. The results were miraculous. In two weeks order was restored and the children started working. I decided that, as the class found communicating with and relating to each other very difficult, I would continue teaching them TA.

Being new to TA, and there being very few books available at that time to use with children in school, I devised my own syllabus of PSHE(C) using TA. I decided to teach the children the actual TA theory, reasoning it would give us a common language with a very specific vocabulary.

The three areas I covered were:

- **creating greater self-awareness** using the TA concepts of egostates and strokes;
- **relating to others** through identifying authentic needs and feelings and introducing transactions; and
- **problem-solving and conflict resolution** using the drama triangle, egostate diagnosis and assertiveness techniques.

As is customary in most primary schools nowadays, I hold regular Sharing Circles with my class. Ideally, they are a daily occurrence, but in practice they are usually held three or four times a week. To institute a Sharing Circle I ask the children to sit in a circle on the carpet. Then I explain that Circle Time is a special time which belongs to them; it is a time for helping us to understand ourselves and to get to know each other. As with all groups, Sharing Circles require rules to enable them to be an effective vehicle for change. The children decide the rules, the teacher's role being to frame the suggestions positively. A maximum of six rules seems to be the optimum number for the success of the group. A typical list of rules might be:

- one person to speak at a time;
- keep your hands and feet to yourself (i.e. don't fight);
- listen carefully and politely to what others are saying;
- it is OK to pass (i.e. not comment during an activity which is going round the circle);
- be punctual for the Sharing Circle; and
- it is OK to feel what you feel.

RACKETS AND REAL FEELINGS

Once the ground rules are established I begin by teaching the children about feelings. TA theory states that there are four *authentic* feelings. They are: mad (angry), scared, sad and glad. Many of the other feelings we experience are called *racket* feelings – such as anxiety, guilt and confusion – and anger, sadness, fear and gladness can sometimes be racket feelings too. Fanita English (1972) writes: 'Rackets are stylised repetitions of permitted feelings which were stroked in the past. They are expressed each time a real feeling (of a different category) is about to surface.' Stewart and Joines (1987) further state: 'We define a racket feeling as a familiar emotion, learned and encouraged in childhood, experienced in many different stress situations, and maladaptive as an adult means of problem solving'. This example shows how this process can begin. In this case the child was able to understand her own feelings and decide to act authentically.

Case study

Helen is being brought up very much in a TA way. Her parents always give her permission to feel what she is feeling. When she was aged 3 she was enrolled in an excellent nursery school. Her parents were very pleased at being able to provide such a high standard of preschool care. However, after about four months they became very distressed as her behaviour had changed for the worse. Helen was always whining and crying, never asking for things that she needed and going around looking sad. It wasn't until I went to collect her from school one day that the mystery was solved. As I sat, unobserved at the back of the room, I noticed that Helen's favourite nursery teacher was paying great attention to a child who was crying, first of all picking up the child and cuddling her, and then, when the sobs had subsided, letting her share her chair during story time. Walking home with Helen I casually mentioned what I had seen. Helen immediately reeled off the advantages of behaving in such a manner with this particular teacher – sharing the chair with her, being cuddled, getting a sweet, being allowed to play with a toy that another child wanted to use, and many other treats. I pointed out that the child had been crying. Helen replied, very matter of factly, that the teacher didn't like you to be sad, so if you were she would cheer you up.

I reported my observations to Helen's parents who dealt with it in a sensitive way. If she started with racket behaviour (e.g. whining) they would remark that if it were them in that situation they would probably feel sad or scared (a feeling appropriate to the moment). When Helen protested and said, 'Well at school I always feel sad', they said it was OK to feel sad at school if she felt she ought to, but that at home she could feel how she wanted, i.e. authentic feelings. Helen's behaviour returned to normal at home and at school; she said it was boring always crying. In another household, if this behaviour was not understood, a child may well have developed a sadness racket.

I teach the children about racket feelings because, as Stewart and Joines (1987) state, racket feelings are not effective in solving problems. Furthermore, a person's authentic feelings are squashed down under the layers of racket feelings; therefore these feelings are not appropriate to the situation. They are also censored in that the person is not able to be spontaneous.

During the first Circle Time on this topic I explain that every person experiences four authentic feelings, and I write them on the board. I explain that having these feelings enables us to be spontaneous, helps us to solve problems, and that they are appropriate to the situation. We then have a *thought shower* as to what one might do or feel when having these feelings. I then explain that, at home, your parents or carers like you to feel certain emotions, and I ask if any child can identify a feeling that is stroked at home. Children often say, 'My mum doesn't like me to be sad, she says be happy'. After some discussion other children will discover that they are encouraged not to be angry and perhaps they are stroked for being sad or depressed.

At this point I stress that it is fine to behave at home how your parents wish you to behave but that at school it is fine to feel what you are feeling and express it appropriately.

Activities using art to allow children to identify feelings

To facilitate children to experience their authentic feelings, or to begin to identify them, I use art and drama activities with great success.

Drawing or painting while listening to music
• Choose a piece of music that is likely to suggest a specific feeling to the children;

- let the children choose their own size piece of paper;
- provide a variety of mark-makers for the children to use (paint, chalk pastels or crayons seem to be the most successful);
- play through the music, the children listening at this point;
- tell the children that next time you play the music you want them to do a picture of the feeling the music creates in them. (I do not do any discussion of what the feelings might be as I have found that children who have trouble accessing their feelings would merely take up the suggestions, or copy someone else's. If they say they do not know what to do, I say 'It doesn't matter, just draw a picture'. More often than not an authentic feeling surfaces or I am able to identify their racket feeling.)

When the pictures are finished the children like to discuss their pictures.

Case study

For two years I taught a girl who was a cared-for child. She did not attend school until the age of 6, and only then because she was found foraging for food in a skip. Her mother was a drug-user who funded her habit through prostitution. Laura was locked in an unlit cupboard while her mother worked or was taken along and put in the corner of the room where her mother worked. Laura had many serious psychological problems and was expelled from two primary schools for unacceptable and dangerous behaviour.

Laura made slow progress, until I did the above activity. Her usual reaction when feelings were mentioned was to shout loudly that she wasn't going to do 'that c—p'. She would then start escalating her behaviour until she had to be removed from the classroom. On this occasion, however, she just chose her piece of paper silently, took a packet of chalk pastels, sat down by herself and drew a picture. After we had finished she said she wanted to show me on my own what she had done. The music that day had been 'In the Hall of the Mountain King', from the Peer Gynt Suite.

Laura said the music had 'reminded her of scare'. She had drawn a picture of a large field with very long grass. A small figure was walking in the grass. In the top corner were two coffins with 'Mum' and 'Dad' written on them. I asked her if she would like to tell me the story of the picture. Laura said, 'A little girl is looking for her mum and dad. She is lost in the jungle grass and she doesn't know yet that they are dead.'

Laura's behaviour changed radically after this experience and she began to identify when she was scared instead of exhibiting racket rage. It also provided her with a safe vehicle within which to explore her feelings, both in the here-and-now and also in the past.

Drama techniques useful in working with feelings
- Audience direct

  In the manner of a film director, the audience directs the actions and responses of the people in role. Children can be given a scenario or a story to act out. The audience, on the second run through, can intervene at any point and ask the character to feel or behave differently. Once when I was using this technique with my class, I had given them the story of Cinderella to change. It was quite slow going until a small boy suggested this intervention: '[I suggest] Cinderella gets off her arse, stops moaning, goes and gets a job and then she can buy her own ball dress'. After that the suggestions came thick and fast.
- Freeze-frame

  The audience can make a signal to stop the action and the 'actors' freeze in the manner of a photograph, sculpture or the freeze-frame on a video. This enables changes to be made or feelings to be explored at any point in the action.
- Thought tracking

  Invite the children to reveal publicly the private thoughts and feelings of their roles at specific moments in the action. In conjunction with this you can ask the character what he had been feeling the previous moment, what he might feel as the scene progresses or what he thinks the cause and effect of this action will be. If the character cannot think of an answer another child is allowed to put the thought or feeling into words.

The use of clay
Clay is another useful commodity when doing work on feelings.

- It can be used to show racket feelings and authentic feelings in the form of a 3D 'Janus' head. (Janus was the Roman god of the New Year who looked back into the past and forward into the future.) Children can make a two-faced head (like Janus), one face showing an authentic feeling and the other a racket feeling.
- Masks can be made showing different types of feelings.
- Just thumping a mass of clay can be cathartic for some children. I usually let them do it until they do not want to do it any more.

Other uses of mark-makers
- By using a stimulus such as a poem or a story, children can access feelings in a safe way. After using the stimulus the children are asked to do a picture of the feeling which has been expressed.
- Drama can be used in conjunction with picture-making. First, use one of the techniques described in the section on drama, then ask the children to capture the feeling in a picture.

Applying the 'feelings' work

Working with anger

In my experience many children think that they are not allowed to show anger in any form. Others are only used to expressing anger in a violent way, so much of my work is about teaching children that it is all right to feel anger but that anger must be expressed in a way that does not harm anyone or damage property. There is a variety of methods that can be used in a primary classroom:

- giving children wodges of newspaper to tear up and throw into a bin;
- scribbling with a thick, black crayon onto newspaper – the harder they press the more satisfactory it is; the child can then tear this up if they wish;
- drawing a picture of what has upset them, or a person who has upset them; they can then scribble over this, shred it up, stamp on it, cut it up or dispose of it how they wish;
- some children prefer to make a loud noise; I give them permission to go outside to stamp, scream, yell and run round the playground until they have got rid of their anger;
- a large floor cushion or beanbag is useful when working with anger. Children, under adult supervision, can take their shoes off and jump, kick or punch the bag. They can hit the beanbag with a plastic bat, they can throw it around the room or they can pretend the person they are cross with, but to whom it isn't safe to tell their feelings, is on the beanbag. They can then tell the person exactly what they think of him or her.

All these activities need to be closely supervised by the teacher or a knowledgeable member of the support staff who stresses to the children that it is not OK to hurt themselves or anyone else or to damage property.

For children who have to be 'good' at home

Some children are not allowed to be boisterous at home; indeed, some children are not allowed to make a noise. For these children I introduced 'silly time'. This took place immediately after lunchtime each day.

- The child chooses a friend to enjoy him/herself with.
- The child then suggests things he/she would like to do.
- The teacher then provides the necessary equipment.
- Each day the child is given 15 minutes after lunch to be silly.
- Suggested props are water pistols, role play clothes, silly string, crazy foam, whoopee cushion, books of jokes, party whistles etc.

The children are supervised, but not directed, by an adult to ensure their safety. They are allowed to be outside the classroom for the agreed 15 minutes.

Death of a family member

The death of a family member is traumatic for an adult, and even more so for a child. Often the child thinks that he/she is to blame for the death or they are confused because they have not been told that the person is dead but has just gone away. Circle Time can be very supportive for a child who is grieving as special activities can be carried out. Some suggestions for grief rituals appropriate for school are:

- Make a book of memories of the person. If possible, start this when they know the person is going to die, so that it can be a book of shared memories. Include photographs and other memorabilia in this.
- Write a letter to the person who is dead (or dying), saying how much you will miss them and what you will specifically miss about them.
- Ask, in the Sharing Circle, what support the child needs. If the child doesn't know, get the other children to make suggestions; the grieving child can then choose.
- Make sure the child has somewhere to go if he/she needs to be private, or to talk quietly to an adult.
- Light a large church candle in the centre of the circle and ask all the children to think about someone they love, or have loved. Ask if there are any volunteers to tell the rest of the circle about that person.
- If there are two children with similar experiences they can support each other in that they soon realise they are not abnormal in the way they are feeling.
- Explain to the children how it is essential for our health that we grieve a loss. Briefly explain the stages of grieving, then the children begin to understand that how they feel is part of the process.
- Allow the child to be sad and to cry.

Grief

Until recently in my teaching career it was thought that children do not understand loss and that therefore they do not need to grieve. This was very much a mistaken idea. I have taught many children who have had unresolved grief issues which have left them unable to learn or relate satisfactorily to other people. It is essential that these issues be acknowledged in school.

Grieving happens whenever there is a loss, not just when someone dies. In the school in which I worked we started grieving a few weeks before the end of the school year. This facilitated the children in their moving to a new class, a new school, a different teacher and sometimes a new set of friends. We did this process in three stages:

- We discussed our triumphs over the last year, and told anecdotes about something which had amused or saddened us. Lots of the children talked about their special times with their friends. I gave strokes to all the children; they gave strokes to me. The children made 'Warm Fuzzy' books in which their friends wrote strokes for them.

- The next stage is to give the children the opportunity to state the things they will miss and that will not be the same next year.
- The final stage is to say how each child will feel next year, what they are afraid of and what they are looking forward to.

Unresolved grief can cause a child innumerable difficulties.

Case study

Warren was seven years old when he came into my class. He had a reputation for destructive, defiant behaviour. He had broken his nursery teacher's nose. When I first met him his behaviour was almost uncontrollable. He was defiant, disruptive and violent. I couldn't see a cause for such extreme behaviour. In conversation with his mother, who was very supportive, I discovered that his father had died when Warren was two years old. She said Warren had been seen by a psychiatrist and had been told he had unresolved grief issues. At the same time, another child in the class (Mel) was grieving over the death of his father from a car crash. Ostensibly working with Mel, I managed to draw Warren into the grieving process. He worked through the stages of grieving, especially the anger he felt. He is an articulate child and eventually was able to verbalise his feelings. He also did lots of anger work, and art helped him identify his feelings. At the end of the year his unacceptable behaviour had gone; he was a happy, healthy boy.

TEACHING STROKES

One of the major improvements to the psychological health of a class is to ensure there is a rich stroking culture. Eric Berne (1964) describes a stroke as 'a unit of human recognition'. Strokes are essential to mental and physical health.
There are four types of strokes:

- positive conditional – for *doing* things correctly;
- positive unconditional – for just *being* you;
- negative conditional – for *doing* something wrong; and
- negative unconditional – negative attention for *being* yourself.

Strokes are so vital to our health that if we don't get the positive strokes we need we will seek to get negative ones. As stroking reinforces behaviour, children will try out different ways of behaving to see which one will get stroked. If there is a lack of strokes in the classroom the behaviour of the children often escalates into uproar. It is essential therefore that stroking becomes embedded into the classroom culture. As all children want strokes this is the easiest concept to teach, so I usually begin my programme by teaching stroke theory first.

I begin by asking what 'to stroke' means. The children readily understand the physical action. Then I ask what or who do we stroke. A child usually volunteers that a mother strokes her baby. At this point I initiate a discussion about appropriate touching, and the children, without fail, decide that they wouldn't like to be physically stroked by most people now they are growing up. The next question I ask is 'How do you get the recognition that you need?' The class find it easy to make a list of ways of giving strokes. At this point I ascertain what type of stroke each child prefers, explaining that if you don't get your preferred type of stroke you tend to discount it. For this I use Worksheet A (Appendix 2).

First, the children learn how to give and receive strokes. This is done in four stages:

- In the Sharing Circle a child chooses another person to give a stroke to. He/she does this in the third person – no eye contact.
- The same child, on another occasion, gives a stroke to someone in the first person with no eye contact.
- The same child, later, gives a stroke in the first person, with eye contact.
- The recipient says 'thank you'.

The children are allowed to say 'no, thank you' if they do not want a stroke. Children are discouraged from discounting a stroke someone has given them.

Another useful aid for teaching strokes is to read *A Fuzzy Tale* by Claude Steiner (1977). This explains stroke theory in an allegorical form.

To reinforce stroking, thereby raising the child's self-esteem still further, there are many activities which do not take a lot of preparation or require expensive equipment:

- Warm Fuzzy book of strokes – already referred to in the grieving process.
- Post Box: this is a class or whole-school activity. Tell the children that you are going to provide a post box (we have a large, red, wooden one at school) and leave it in an accessible position for a week. During that week the children can write a stoke on a postcard to a friend. The postcards are delivered the following week (Worksheet B, Appendix 2).
- Children make a stroke tally over the course of one day of all the strokes they have received.
- Organise a 'stroking circle'. Children sit in a circle and give a stroke to the next person (make sure you place yourself in front of a person who may not receive any strokes).
- If a child is stroke-deprived, place them in the centre of the circle and ask each child to give them a stroke until they have received enough.
- For younger children, a Birthday Board works on the same principle. When a child has a birthday his/her name and photograph go on the special board. The teacher scribes the other students' strokes for the special person. These are presented to him at the end of the day. During the day he will have special privileges.

TEACHING EGOSTATES

Teaching the children egostate theory enhances their self-awareness and helps them understand the behaviour of others. Eric Berne defined an egostate as 'a consistent pattern of feeling and experience directly related to a corresponding pattern of behaviour' (Berne 1964). I teach egostate theory using the basic egostate model (Figure 1.1) and a Russian Matruschka doll (nesting doll). The doll is useful as it demonstrates that inside each of us we have 'sets of feelings and experiences'. As I take the doll apart I discuss what might be the behaviour and experiences of someone who was in this egostate. To aid visual learners I then draw the basic model on a flipchart and invite the class to have a thought shower about the behaviours and words we might see for each egostate. The flipchart is left on display in the classroom.

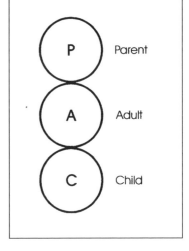

Figure 1.1: Egostate diagram (Berne 1961)

I teach the class that Parent and Child egostates can be subdivided, and introduce the functional model (Figure 1.2). We then have a further thought shower.

To enable the children to be able to identify egostates, and to experience being in different egostates, I use a variety of activities:

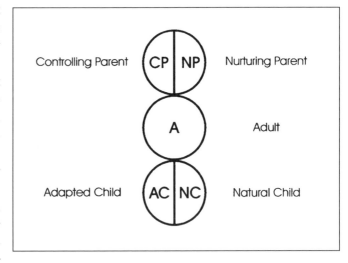

Figure 1.2: Functional egostate diagram (Berne 1961)

- draw themselves in each ego state or do a pen picture (Worksheet C, Appendix 2);
- make a huge composite egostate diagram with each child adding his/her own picture or words;
- in the Sharing Circle, have envelopes available with a scenario which has to be acted in a certain egostate (Worksheet D, Appendix 2);
- give the children scenarios in which the child has to shift egostate;
- to help children identify the different egostates I sometimes take in a video of a 'soap'.

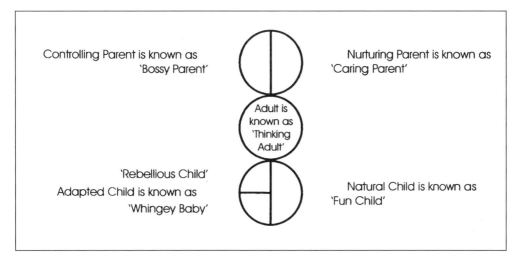

Figure 1.3: Children's names for egostates

I explain that the aim is not to be in Adult all the time but to be in the appropriate egostate for the situation. It is worth clarifying that Adult does not equate with being grown-up.

Some classes I have taught have given the egostates their own terminology (see Figure 1.3) This seems to help their understanding. Other classes use a dictionary to find out the definition 'critical' and 'nurturing', and are able to use the correct terminology.

During one Ofsted inspection an inspector was just walking out of the door when a child announced loudly 'I'm glad he's gone; he was in right Bossy Parent'. He was!

Once the children understand this theory and are able to apply it, they respond to invitations such as 'Will you please move into Adult', or questions such as 'Which egostate do you need to be in now?' The behaviour in the class alters as each child becomes responsible for his/her own behaviour. If the children are not behaving appropriately I only have to make a statement such as 'If you don't tidy up properly I will have to move into Bossy Parent' for them to shift into the appropriate egostate. Also, at playtime, they can identify that sometimes discord is caused by someone being in an inappropriate egostate. One child actually said to me 'I was in Whingey Baby, so I hit him back first'.

CONCLUSION

Following the success of using TA with that first class I have taught relevant TA concepts throughout the primary age range. Over the last 20 years I have found that the use of TA in the classroom has improved behaviour, which in turn has led to a more conducive learning environment, thereby raising self-esteem and academic standards. I have also seen how TA has helped children with particular social and emotional challenges to resolve their difficulties.

In summary the results of teaching TA in the primary school classroom are:

- raised self-esteem;
- children controlling their own behaviour;
- pupils becoming more emotionally literate and better communicators;
- children having a tool to aid conflict resolution; and
- children having greater self-awareness.

2

Saying Hello: Establishing a Pastoral Mentoring Service in an Inner-city Secondary School

PETE SHOTTON

INTRODUCTION

In 1999 the UK government developed its programme of social inclusion in education (DfEE 1999). One of the first tangible developments was the Excellence in Cities initiative. Money was made available to schools in seven metropolitan authorities in order to address issues of disaffection, underachievement and exclusion in inner-city schools. The guidance was suggesting that schools should set up and staff initiatives for inclusion based around two strands, one of which was the development of on-site units for targeted pupils, the other the appointment of a new body of workers called Learning Mentors. At the time I was working as a peripatetic support teacher for pupils with dyslexia and I was in transactional analysis training. I was interested in this new development, especially the Learning Mentor role, as I saw in it an opportunity for me to use my experience in education and TA together in a new and exciting field.

The school that appointed me asked me for ideas based on my work with pupils who were often seen as disaffected and disenfranchised. Together we negotiated my job description and the provision that we would offer. I started working at the school in October 1999. It is an inner-city boys' high school with a population of 1,100 boys aged 11 to 16. At that time 74 per cent of the boys were from minority ethnic backgrounds, 58 per cent were Muslim and the school had the highest percentage of children receiving free school meals (68 per cent) of any high school in the city.

INCLUSION

The main thrust of my work and that of my team is to provide a pastoral support framework which is open and available to all pupils. This is based on my belief that inclusion encompasses provision for all. Many Learning Mentor job descriptions and much of the early guidance in 1999 (10/99) (DfEE 1999:8) mentioned working with targeted groups of pupils who were usually identified as having behavioural problems. The guidance was not prescriptive but many schools treated it as such, with the effect that access to Mentor support was limited and exclusive, in that it was for a labelled group rather than being inclusive, accessible to all and offering a range of differentiated support appropriate to individual needs. We are easily accessible to all of the boys in our school and, as a result of this policy, culture problems are identified and addressed within the school at an earlier stage than they would have been in the past.

Within the school structure I am classed as having a middle-management post. This puts me on a level with heads of faculty and heads of year. My team is part of a wider inclusion faculty which is managed by an assistant head teacher who is my line manager. However, given the all-encompassing nature of the support that we offer, I work closely with all members of the middle management and the leadership team of head teacher, deputy head teachers and assistant head teachers.

Shortly after commencing at the school, I wrote a policy statement describing our work. I wrote 'we work with any boys in school who have identified themselves, or have been identified by teachers or parents/carers, as having personal issues or concerns that may prevent them from getting the most out of school'. This message is proactively transmitted on posters in school, in flyers that are sent out to parents and through presentations in school assemblies.

We each work with boys, individually or in groups, offering counselling, mediation, self-esteem work, anger management, peer mentoring training and catch-up sessions for boys who are struggling with coursework. We do not have a formal referral process. Boys can refer themselves to us directly, and to ensure that this can happen we are always on the corridors or the play areas at breaks and lunchtime, initiating and responding to contact. During the school year we expect to work with at least a third of the school's population.

TA AND MENTORING

One of the reasons that I was able to successfully introduce and establish mentoring within the school system was that I had, in TA, a philosophical framework and an array of tools and strategies for facilitating change and growth. I demonstrated this through the contracting process and through my ability to implement and explain effective interventions. Once my team was appointed I ran a short training session explaining the fundamental assumptions of TA and negotiating our goals as a team using contracting as a structure.

None of the team had any previous experience of TA, and as part of their own professional development they opted to undertake further TA training, with two of them completing an introductory TA course at a local training institute. The other member of the team, together with two teaching assistants who were interested in the way we worked, completed an evening course on TA core concepts at a local university.

I use TA in my work with the boys. Using the functional model of egostates I introduce an awareness of behaviours, theirs and others, how they react to them and how they can change. I also use contracts, life positions, strokes and games. My aims in using TA in this context are:

- to enable the boys to recognise the potential they have, and the part they play, in making changes to achieve the best for themselves during their time at school;
- to enable the boys to recognise the choices that they have, and that they make, both inside and outside school; and
- to support and help the boys in making changes and positive choices for themselves.

These aims are taken from a leaflet which I produced for circulation to pupils, parents and teachers. Teaching staff have begun to express an interest in the work that I have done with the boys and I have recently set up a peer support group for staff where we discuss relationships in the classroom and where I offer a TA perspective.

THE SCHOOL CULTURE

When I began working as a Mentor, I was part of the creation of a new cultural subgroup in school and was aware that, therefore, I and my team would be affecting the cultural scripting of the organisational structure in which we worked. Cultural scripting is defined by White and White (1975:171) as 'that set of reinforcements or limitations established by the Parent values embodied in the institutions of a culture'.

In the school, we encountered generalised script messages which were, and are, applied to the wide variety of cultural subgroups within our multicultural setting. The school has a population drawn from 25 different countries of origin with 28 languages other than, or as well as, English, spoken at home or in the community. Generalised beliefs, which have been voiced by boys, parents and teachers, include 'Asian boys stick together in their family and community and work hard in school', 'Somali boys are always smiling and never fight each other', 'Black African/ Caribbean boys are more than likely going to be involved in [criminal] gangs' and 'The only white boys we get here are the ones whose families are too poor or don't care enough to send them elsewhere'. These statements will confirm different, and often negative, script beliefs for the individuals making them. This process is described by Roberts (1975:189) in the following way:

the ongoing external stress of a person's societal situation distorts what is figural and what is ground to the individual. When this occurs, persons are oppressed and limited and they, outside of their awareness, structure situations and events that reinforce their figure/ground 'stuckness'. Cultural, ethnic, sexual, family, social class and provincial scripts interlock with the personal life scripts . . .

In their article 'Cultural scripting', White and White describe and model the way that cultural scripting can change in a 'therapeutic community', that is a community where 'change in human behaviour that is rooted in counterscript and script can occur in a co-ordinated programme that includes a culture that supports the direction of change and that confronts consistently the unwanted behaviours' (p.180). I see mentoring as part of that process of confrontation and change.

Case study

When we first started working in the school we were based on the lower school part of a split site. The school was to move on to a single site, the upper school site, within a few weeks. I went to have a look around the site and to check out possible places that boys might go to if they were truanting from lessons, as that was a significant problem at that time. As I approached a stairwell at the back of the school I saw somebody in a hooded top smoking. He was taller and broader than me and I realised that he could be an intruder or he could be one of the boys. I considered walking in the opposite direction because I felt scared and unsure of myself. Then I thought to myself, 'He might be feeling as unsure and scared as me', and I walked up to him, held out my hand and said, 'Hi, I'm Pete, I've just started working here with a new team called the Mentors. Who are you?' He dropped his cigarette, which meant that he was most likely a pupil, looked at my hand, cautiously shook it, and said, 'I'm Danny'. I told him about the team and he told me about himself. He was a Year 11 boy who rarely attended school and only really came in to see his mates. He had given up on taking any exams. He felt school had nothing left to offer him and that it was better for all concerned that he didn't go to lessons. He would only argue with the teachers and get in the way of others learning. I went back and discussed this encounter with my team and two decisions came about as a result of our discussion. One was that we would actively initiate contact with everybody we encountered in school and the other was that we would actively seek out and work with boys who had given up on themselves. Since that time we always say hello to everybody we meet on the corridor. Danny left school with a G grade for Food Technology which, as he pointed out, was one more than he'd been expecting to get when he met me.

CULTURAL CHANGE

In introducing mentoring into schools the policy-makers in education were confronting script messages in schools which denied the potency of the school–pupil relationship. These messages would be voiced in phrases such as 'We only see them for six out of 24 hours' or 'We're not Social Workers' when presented with issues concerning pupil welfare. These phrases, and the attitudes they represent, could be seen as reflecting injunctions such as 'Don't Be You', 'Don't Be Important', 'Don't Be Close' and the driver, 'Be Strong'. Within the culture, this can lead to commonly held beliefs such as the one I often encountered when I first started in my job – 'Teenage boys don't like to talk about their feelings'.

This belief has been confronted and updated through the work of my team, with boys actively seeking emotional support and teachers acknowledging that they have an impact on their relationships with pupils. In my training programme I was aiming to reinforce the process of confronting and changing cultural script messages by offering a potent, practical alternative. In Figure 2.1, I have adapted a model of change procedures in cultural scripting (White and White 1975) as a template to show the impact of mentoring on the cultural script in schools. When I began the process of putting the training programme together I talked through this model with members of my team, explaining the transactions and filling them in as I talked. They were enthusiastic about this diagram as a vehicle for understanding and explaining our impact.

1. Cultural scripting

The ongoing process of working together to support change, to question and confront outdated values and to choose and reinforce an appropriate value system for our working setting. Our value system is informed by the fundamental principles of TA:

- People are OK
- People can think and therefore make choices
- People can change.

These statements are on display in the rooms that we work in and are modelled by us in our interactions with others. One transaction that we use and encourage staff to use when confronting challenging behaviour is, 'This is not about who you are, it is about the way you are behaving right now'.

2. Updating the Parent

Sharing and modelling the changing values, manifested in the way that we initiate contact and conduct ourselves in school. A member of my team would introduce

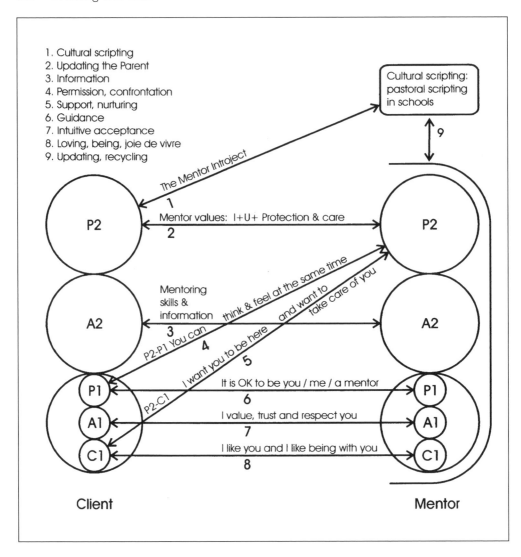

1. Cultural scripting
2. Updating the Parent
3. Information
4. Permission, confrontation
5. Support, nurturing
6. Guidance
7. Intuitive acceptance
8. Loving, being, joie de vivre
9. Updating, recycling

Cultural scripting:
pastoral scripting
in schools

The Mentor Introject

Mentor values: I+U+ Protection & care

Mentoring skills & information   think & feel at the same time   and want to take care of you

P2-P1 You can

I want you to be here

P2-C1

It is OK to be you / me / a mentor

I value, trust and respect you

I like you and I like being with you

Client

Mentor

Figure 2.1: Cultural script diagram for mentoring (adapted from White and White 1975)

herself to a new pupil in the following way: 'Hi, I'm June. I'm part of the mentoring team here in school. We're a team of people employed by the school to offer you support for dealing with any things that might be bothering you and stopping you from getting the most out of school. You'll see us around school and if you want to talk you can ask us yourself or you can ask your form teacher to arrange for you to see one of the team. You choose who you want to talk to.' All new boys are introduced to the team this way. The message is regularly reinforced by us speaking to form groups and year group assemblies.

3. Information

Providing information (TA theory) and evidence (data collection), which fits the Parent values and satisfies and supports the Child needs and wants. I keep records of all our contact and provide annual summative reports for governors and staff and the LEA. Within the reports I write mini case studies describing and reinforcing the impact of our work.

4. Permission, confrontation

The investing of Parent energy in promoting appropriate behaviours with potency and consistency. We often deal with boys who have been involved in fights. Recently a boy who was very angry was telling me that he was going to go out and find the boy who had hit him and that he was going to 'smash his face in'. I told him that I understood that he felt really angry and pointed out that I could not stop him from doing what he intended to do. I then said, 'However, before you go I want you to tell me what the consequences will be and that you understand and are willing to accept those consequences'. In doing this I was acknowledging his feelings of hurt and injustice and I was inviting him to think and to recognise his choices. He did not go after the other boy but, instead, stayed and processed his feelings, and later allowed us to mediate and resolve the issue with the other boy.

5. Support, nurturing

The investing of Parent energy in promoting care, protection and acceptance. We will often meet boys who are not used to being accepted, boys for whom the message 'You are not wanted here' has been made explicit at home and/or at school. Their belief that they are unacceptable will mean that they will try to push away or reject our support by acting out. Whenever they walk away, or push us away we always tell them that they are welcome to come back and that we will be there to offer them support when they do. We continue to consistently recognise them around school, saying hello whenever we see them, until the day that they choose to initiate contact and, by accepting us, begin to find themselves acceptable.

6. Guidance

Acceptance of self, the other and our roles.

7. Intuitive acceptance

A feeling and bond of trust reinforced by the feeling of Child-to-Child acceptance.

8. Loving, being, *joie de vivre*

Acceptance of self and the others' feelings.

Transactions 6, 7 and 8 refer to the interpersonal relationships between us and our clients and therefore emphasise the importance of these one-to-one exchanges in creating and maintaining the cultural script. They are expressed through transactions like, 'What do you think would be a good solution?' or 'Will you teach me how to do that' or 'You tell me about 50 Cent and I'll tell you about James Brown' or 'I really like that hat and we've agreed that because of school rules we don't wear hats in here' or 'It's great talking to you', all of which form the building blocks for mutually accepting, respectful and enjoyable relationships.

I have introduced the Mentor role as an introject and have added the frame and arrow (9) encompassing and connecting the Mentor to cultural scripting. White and White represent the cultural scripting box as cultural Parent (Pc) values, which is why I have represented the Mentor role as a proactive cultural Parental introject.

The frame and vector (9) represent the Mentor as an Integrated Adult, as suggested by Berne (1961), and described by Erskine (1988:16) as having the qualities of 'emotional, cognitive and moral development; the ability to be creative; and the capacity for full contactful engagement in meaningful relationships'. I also wanted to show cultural scripting as an ongoing process, constantly being updated and developed in the light of new co-created information. I see the idea of co-creativity as crucial when looking at the cultural scripting process, and I am informed by Summers and Tudor (2000: 24) and their summary of the principles of constructivism that are relevant to co-creational TA:

- meaning constantly evolves through dialogue;
- discourse creates systems (and not the other way around);
- therapy is the co-creation, in dialogue, of new narratives that provide new possibilities; and
- the therapist (Mentor) is a participant-observer in this dialogue.

Case study

A member of the team recently left to take up a new post. On his last day I asked if he would like to say goodbye to the boys in the school assembly. He stood up and told the boys about their impact on him; about the beliefs that he had come into the job with as an Afro-Caribbean man who had not done as well as he could in school; about the perceptions that he and colleagues and boys had shared in seeing him as a big, hard man who would be good at breaking up fights; and about the way that he had changed alongside the boys in learning to talk more about feelings in the groups that we ran. He saw himself in a different light and he knew that others could see this. He thanked the boys for their willingness to work and change and grow alongside him. At the end of the assembly, boys who would normally present a tough-guy persona in school came up to him and hugged him and cried, and throughout his last day, teachers found him and said how much he had helped them change the way they saw themselves and the boys.

Through using TA models to provide a common language and a structural-analytical framework we have been able to confront and work with interlocking cultural and personal life-scripts and are continuing to co-create new narratives.

3

It Doesn't Matter What Age You Are – It's What Stage You Are At That Counts

GILL WONG and EMMA BRADSHAW

This chapter will describe how the theory of the Cycle of Development (Levin 1982) and the use of developmental affirmations (Clarke and Dawson 1998) have been used as tools for assessing and attending to children's emotional needs, using case studies of two children as a focus. In so doing, the chapter will tell several stories:

- the story of a nursery school struggling to maintain and include a child whose behaviour presented significant challenges to the staff, children and parents at the school;
- the story of the child himself and of the learning experienced by the adults who came together to support him; and
- the story of a high school pupil whose chronological age and academic ability masked his need to indulge in some early childhood experiences in order to change what were considered by his teachers to be silly and irritating behaviours.

Case study: a chance to thrive – enabling change in a nursery school[1]

We were asked by the head teacher of a nursery school to provide in-service training (INSET) for her staff on the stages of development in order to help them in dealing with the wide range of behaviours of the children they were looking after. During this day we spent a morning with the head teacher and key workers at the nursery discussing the school's response to a handful of children who were causing particular concern. The child causing most concern was a boy who had been placed recently at the nursery by Social Services.

---

1 This case study of Nathan has been published previously, with TA analysis and commentary, as an article in *Transactional Analysis Journal* (Newton and Wong 2003).

We used a framework to look at the behaviours of this child as a preliminary to exploring his needs for healthy development. The framework prescribed a pooling of experience and knowledge about this child, which we put onto a flipchart within these headings:

* Age of the child
* Behaviours observed – both positive and problematical
* Any background known about the child's earlier and current experiences at home or elsewhere
* Strategies already tried to support him, both successful and unsuccessful.

As we went through the process of pooling information we developed a portrait of this child, and the process of setting down information onto one large 'map' gave us some clear and explicit (albeit complex) problems on which to focus.

The results, a year on, were found to be significantly positive, not only for the child, his family, the school and the whole-school community, but also in providing proof of the effectiveness of systemic behaviour support work, a child deficit based approach.

Nathan's story

Nathan was aged 3 years, 10 months. His placement in the nursery was for the summer term only, after which he would be placed elsewhere, possibly in a mainstream reception class or, if it was felt that his needs were too severe, in a special school.

Nathan's behaviour in the nursery

Nathan had very limited language, with few and indistinct spoken words, echoing the last one or two words spoken to him, and he appeared to have little understanding of what was said to him by adults or children. The staff observed that he repeated words relating to objects he saw in the sky. The nursery had worked hard to increase his language and felt he had made considerable progress in this area, to the extent that he was beginning to remember and use some words, although he rarely initiated verbal communication. That he had made progress was a major factor in sustaining the nursery in its determination to find more time and ways to help him.

Nathan never smiled, although he would laugh as he ran away when staff tried to approach him if he had hurt another child or had done something which required a boundary to be enforced. On these occasions he would tug on his ears as if to turn them off and look back to see if he was going to be chased, appearing to invite staff into a cat-and-mouse game. His responses to other children were largely aggressive (hitting, pinching or snatching from them if they had something he wanted). He flinched when adults approached him suddenly and he resisted any touch, becoming violent if adult interventions were needed, for instance to prevent him from hurting himself or other children. Nathan never sought help if he injured himself and appeared to feel no physical pain or to show emotion. He showed little interest in interacting with children or adults unless it was to disturb or hurt them.

Nathan walked in a stooped posture, his arms hanging by his sides, palms facing backwards and fingers curled up, head down with no facial contact. He had rapid, jerky movements and walked on his toes. His body was rigid and stiff, and he avoided physical contact. He soiled and wet himself many times each day, showing no signs of realising he had done so, in spite of staff trying many strategies such as asking him if he needed the toilet or taking him and sitting him on the toilet at regular intervals, and he violently resisted attempts of staff to change his clothes and clean him up.

Nathan was seldom still. He repeated many restless behaviours, would drive bicycles and cars at other children, slammed doors repeatedly and would often throw toys around. He would sweep things off tables onto the floor. The staff observed that one of his favourite things to throw was the small, coloured plastic pegs from a board game. He would do this repeatedly, and at first they thought this was done in temper, but on closer observation they realised that he enjoyed the sensation of watching and feeling the pegs falling around him and bouncing off the floor. He frequently flooded the toilet area by turning on all the taps and watching the water overflow from the basins. This, together with his repeated dwelling in puddles and rain, led them to realise that he had a fascination with water.

The staff found themselves devoting a great deal of time and energy to cleaning up after Nathan, and struggling to keep him and his clothes clean and dry. This aspect of caring for him was particularly draining and frustrating for them.

When we looked at these behaviours as a whole, we arrived at the impression that Nathan had little sense of his own body and its boundaries but that he had a strong urge to explore sensations.

Socially, Nathan appeared to live in his own world. He was uninterested in inter-acting with other children and adults, rarely initiating positive contact. He resisted encouragement to listen, share or contribute to small groups, preferring to play with trains on his own, which he refused adamantly to share with other children.

Nathan's behaviour presented a picture of a child who had few social or emo-tional skills and who rarely showed enjoyment or recognition of anything beyond his own inner world. It was difficult to resist the thought that his needs were so great that there was little that could be done beyond what the nursery staff had

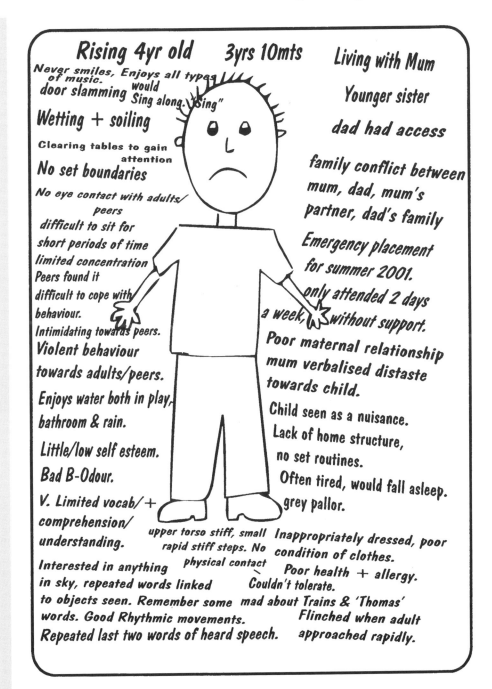

Figure 3.1: Nursery pen portrait of Nathan at 3 years 10 months

already provided for him. However, in hearing their genuine concern for his future, we reminded them of the progress he had made since joining them, and urged them to focus on his enjoyment of music, water and his interest in things he saw in the sky.

In developing this portrait, some themes were emerging which suggested the need for revisiting early stages in his Cycle of Development. However, the bigger picture of how his behaviours were impacting on the nursery, and knowledge of his earlier experiences, needed to be taken into account for us to be able to find a structure for reinforcing their considerable efforts to support Nathan and to find a way forward in making sense of what they had achieved so far. His need for order – although it felt chaotic to the nursery staff – was interpreted by them to be a strong need for routine and structure, all of which were, evidently, absent in his home life.

Nathan's home background
Nathan lived with his mother, who was separated from his father, and his younger sister. His father had access to the children. His father had learning, language and literacy difficulties, as well as alcohol and anger management issues. It was believed that there had been violence in the home. Nathan's mother seemed uninterested in the school's attempts to share their concerns with her and the school, in turn, felt unsupported by her. Her attitude to Nathan was openly negative. Nathan's father appeared to be more supportive of the school, but he had limited access to the children. After Nathan had had access to his father it was noticeable that his behaviour in the nursery was particularly difficult to manage. Nathan's appearance suggested neglect: his skin was pale and he had untreated eczema, and he was tired much of the time. There were few or no boundaries or routines at home and no set time for meals or bed. Nathan was often late for school or did not attend at all, which added to the nursery's frustrations in trying to develop some routines and continuity for him.

The nursery's story
In spite of the improvement in Nathan's language in only three months, staff were feeling that his behaviour was so extreme and his needs so complex that anything they could do for him would be a drop in the ocean, which left them feeling over-whelmed and unsure what to do. They also felt demoralised by the lack of any positive response to their support from Nathan's family.

In addition, his difficulties were having a significant impact on other children attending the nursery. Nathan's aggression and inability to interact positively with other children had caused several injuries to other children, with the result that the children were frightened of him and felt intimidated by him. Several parents had told their children not to go near him, or to hit back at him, and the school was increasingly coming under pressure from parents to exclude him. We were concerned to find a way for the nursery to fully recognise the significant progress they had made with this child, and to suggest strategies that they would not feel were too daunting for them. By piecing together what was known of Nathan's past and current family situation, some likely explanations for his behaviour were suggested. Although these had been evident previously to the nursery in their attempts to work in partnership with Nathan's mother, the process of making them explicit and part of the big picture of his world gave a clarity to the staff as to how they felt about him, as well as revealing some possible ways forward.

Assessment of Nathan's emotional needs
Since Nathan's behaviours were so varied, we used the technique of scaling or scoring tasks within the developmental stages which his behaviours suggested he may need to revisit or which he may be trying to achieve. This indicated that he had not achieved any of the tasks in the Being stage, but that he may be attempting to achieve some of the tasks in the Doing stage.

Nathan's first months of life may have included few helpful responses to his emotional and physical needs, and his lack of interest in his own body, poor self-awareness, poor understanding of body language and limited emotional awareness might all be accounted for by a failure to succeed in these developmental tasks earlier in his life. The following developmental tasks were felt to be a high priority to target:

- to call for care;
- to cry or otherwise signal to get needs met; and
- to accept nurture.

In addition, Nathan's fascination with water, falling pegs, the sky, dance and music, suggested that some support for him in approaching the following tasks would be helpful:

- to explore and experience the environment; and
- to develop sensory awareness by using all senses.

We then looked at which affirmations would be helpful in supporting Nathan in achieving these tasks, and prioritised:

- you can feel all of your feelings;
- what you need is important to us;
- we want you to be here and we want to care for you;
- you can explore and experiment, and we will support and protect you;
- you can do things as many times as you need to;
- you can use all of your senses when you explore; and
- you can be interested in everything.

In view of Nathan's language difficulties, it was felt that the affirmations would be most effectively given to him in as many visual and sensory forms as possible, and the group spent some time developing strategies that could be used by the school's staff to give him the messages that they felt would be helpful to him. It was agreed that all staff would be made aware of the focus of the work to be done with Nathan in order to support his key worker with these strategies.

Prioritising strategies for staff

In order to affirm Nathan in experiencing all his feelings, the nursery would begin toilet-training, as for an infant, using nappies and progressing to using a potty and then a toilet, and Nathan would be encouraged to smell, hear and feel the process of using the toilet. Staff would look out for minor injuries and fuss over him, drawing his attention to which part of his body was hurting. Staff would gradually and carefully increase physical contact with Nathan in as many positive ways as they could.

To encourage Nathan to begin to value his needs, staff would provide him with frequent and routine nurture, such as food, hands and face-washing, and his attention would be drawn to feelings of hunger, enjoyment of food and taste, and other physical sensations. Nathan would be encouraged to cry or call out for attention, and adults would respond quickly and appropriately to this. He would be praised and rewarded for requesting care or nurture. In addition, all caring and nurturing approaches to Nathan would be accompanied by explanations of what the workers were doing and why, in order to show that they wanted to care for him.

Nathan's daily activities were targeted specifically to developing his awareness of his body, and his emotional and sensory feelings. His key worker would concentrate on providing regular and frequent water-play sessions (away from the bathroom); she would use exaggerated facial and verbal expressions to develop his understanding of emotional and physical sensations; and, whenever possible, his own language, words and intonation would be reflected back to him, with the use of actions, pictures and real objects to help extend his understanding and language. Activities such as drawing round his body, hands and feet, looking at and exploring his reflection in a long mirror, with encouragement to explore his face and skin with his hands, and games and activities which involved multisensory experiences were scheduled: dancing without shoes; touching the grass, earth and trees; lying on his back and looking at and talking about birds, planes and insects; sand and mud play; finger painting; kneading playdough. Whenever he was required to sit, his place would be marked out, and he would have ownership of certain toys at certain times, with the reward of going to a special cupboard to get the train out at a pre-arranged time. Music, dancing and rhythmic repetition featured highly as part of his programme.

Many of these strategies were already being used by the nursery, and most of the activities and games were part of the normal curriculum for all children. However, in developing these clear priorities for Nathan and the staff, it was noted by all the staff present that they had a much clearer understanding of what they had been trying to give Nathan on an informal basis, and why. In being explicit about these strategies and why they were linked to specific emotional needs, they felt affirmed in what they had been trying to do for Nathan and enthusiastic and positive about what to do with him in the future. It was evident to us that their sense of confusion and concern was less acute now that they had a plan for moving forward.

A new story for Nathan

Seven months later, Gill contacted the head teacher to see how things were going in the nursery and enquired particularly about Nathan. Her response was unreservedly enthusiastic and Gill was invited back immediately to hear about Nathan's progress. We were touched to find that she and her staff had spent some considerable time showing the Before and After story (Figures 3.1, 3.2).

We sat on the floor, looking at the two large sheets of paper on which the detail of Nathan's story was told. Momentous changes had occurred, and it unfolded that these changes had far-reaching implications, not only for Nathan, but also for his father and sister, the school staff, other children in the school and for their parents and families.

Nathan's achievements

Nathan's language and vocabulary had gone from strength to strength. He knows and uses the names of the other children and adults in the school. He initiates spontaneous verbal contact, listens to instructions and acts appropriately. He approaches adults if he is distressed and seeks support and comfort. He talks about home and life experiences and shows a range of feelings. He accepts boundaries if given notice of them, and he is beginning to share and take turns with other children. His body is now supple and positively responsive to touch. Toileting

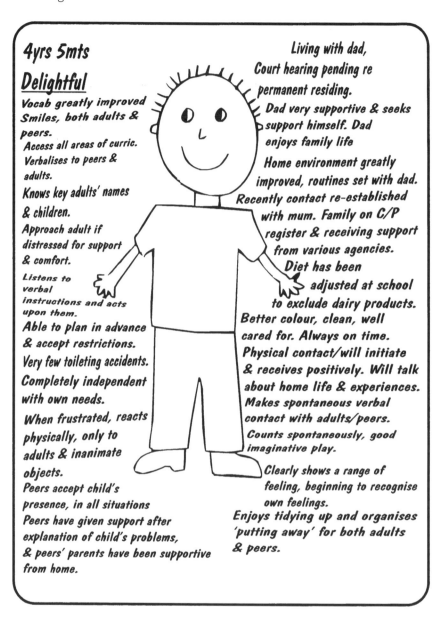

4yrs 5mts

Delightful

Vocab greatly improved
Smiles, both adults &
peers.
Access all areas of curric.
Verbalises to peers &
adults.
Knows key adults' names
& children.
Approach adult if
distressed for support
& comfort.
Listens to verbal
instructions and acts
upon them.
Able to plan in advance
& accept restrictions.
Very few toileting accidents.
Completely independent
with own needs.
When frustrated, reacts
physically, only to
adults & inanimate
objects.
Peers accept child's
presence, in all situations
Peers have given support after
explanation of child's problems,
& peers' parents have been supportive
from home.

Living with dad,
Court hearing pending re
permanent residing.
Dad very supportive & seeks
support himself. Dad
enjoys family life
Home environment greatly
improved, routines set with dad.
Recently contact re-established
with mum. Family on C/P
register & receiving support
from various agencies.
Diet has been
adjusted at school
to exclude dairy products.
Better colour, clean, well
cared for. Always on time.
Physical contact/will initiate
& receives positively. Will talk
about home life & experiences.
Makes spontaneous verbal
contact with adults/peers.
Counts spontaneously, good
imaginative play.
Clearly shows a range of
feeling, beginning to recognise
own feelings.
Enjoys tidying up and organises
'putting away' for both adults
& peers.

Figure 3.2: Nursery pen portrait of Nathan at 4 years 5 months

accidents are very rare. He has found ways of measuring days: if he asks when certain events will happen – for instance, at weekends, asking 'When will I see you again?' – he is reassured by the response of 'After three sleeps'. He smiles often, and attends nursery regularly with enjoyment. He enjoys all areas of the curriculum enthusiastically, and he has particular responsibilities, which he enjoys, including organising the children and adults in tidying up at the end of activities. He has a regular day and time each week for playing with the train. At that time (on the dot!), Nathan goes to the train cupboard, gets it out and begins to build the track. The nursery floor is transformed into a network of increasingly complex and elaborate track schemes on which Nathan and the other children play together. The other children are no longer frightened of him, and he has some close and rewarding friendships among the children. He is felt by everyone in the nursery – children, staff and other parents alike – to be delightful and he is much loved.

Changes in Nathan's home life – his father's achievements
Nathan's father was awarded temporary custody of him and his sister soon after our first visit to the nursery. The reality of having responsibility for his family, and the need for a structure and routines in order to function as a family, gave Nathan's father the strength to seek support and help for his own difficulties. He has made significant changes to his lifestyle and has established a mutually loving and reward- ing home life with his children. His physical and emotional difficulties have been largely overcome. He is calm and caring towards the children, and he has an ongoing and supportive relationship with the school. He has been attending a parent support group and has gained and given much support. He greatly enjoys the experience of being within a family, and is gaining confidence daily, sharing his concerns for Nathan's welfare and future with the school, as would any other parent. Nathan's mother has access to the children, after which his behaviour becomes more difficult, but the school prepares for this and continues to provide a nurturing structure for him. A decision about longer-term custody arrangements for the children is pending.

A new chapter for the school
The school's perspective on Nathan and its role in supporting him and his father is evident from this story. However, there is another aspect in which the school has played a significant part in Nathan's story. Under siege from other parents to exclude Nathan from the nursery at the beginning of this period, the head teacher decided to share with them, sensitively, the reasons why the school wanted to keep Nathan with them, and explained how they planned to support him and what they were trying to achieve. Perhaps surprisingly, in the light of the parents' strong

feelings about Nathan's aggressive behaviour towards their own children, their response to hearing about Nathan's emotional needs was warm and supportive. Several of them commented that they felt fortunate to have children who did not have such acute needs as did Nathan, and many of them asked how they could help him, his family and the school. Gradually, the view that Nathan was bullying their children and getting away with it was diminished. Parents took time to explain to their children what was happening and how they could respond helpfully to Nathan, and the feelings of both children and parents began to change. The school helped the children to find different ways of interacting with Nathan, and parents supported the school in this approach. Nathan became accepted as just another child who belonged in school with all the other children. Parents have generously acknowledged that learning about Nathan and his family was an important event in their own lives and the lives of their children, which has enriched them. This feeling is strongly echoed by all the staff at the nursery. In my conversations with the head teacher, an enduring and heartfelt theme is 'We have learned so much from Nathan. He has taught us so much about ourselves.'

Postscript

A final decision about Nathan's home placement was resolved by a court custody case, and his father has been awarded custody of the children. Nathan left the nursery and took up a place in the Opportunity Base of one of the borough's main-stream schools, following close liaison with the nursery staff who had given Nathan such a supportive start to his education. Nathan will continue to need much support, and the demands of school life will be significant challenges to Nathan and his family. The school he moved on to have many children with a high level of emotional, social and learning needs, of which Nathan is just one. On the strength of experience since our visit to the nursery, there is much important learning to be continued, not least for our team.

RESTORING EMOTIONAL DEVELOPMENT IN HIGH SCHOOL

Nathan's story illustrates how the team's collaborative approach to problem-solving in schools through 'hands-on' training sessions that focus on the needs of the school can have unexpected and far-reaching consequences. It demonstrates that schools need not despair when faced with children whose early or ongoing home experiences may have significantly affected their social behaviour. A further story, this time of a boy in Year 9 of a high school, demonstrates that the stage of development framework can be very effectively applied to children (and adults) of all ages. This optimistic model celebrates the lifelong and organic nature of emotional development and enables us to encourage healthy emotional growth in each other.

Case study: James's story

Emma was invited to deliver a one-hour session on 'Understanding Behaviour' to a staff meeting in a high school. The short amount of time allocated to such a wide subject indicated the relative importance placed by the Senior Management Team on behaviour as opposed to curriculum matters. The school is a high-achieving and standards-focused high school. Faced with the daunting task of covering meaningful ground in such a short time, she opted to give them a brief overview on the Cycle of Development model. Following this session, the head of Year 9 approached Emma and told her about a boy who had been a big problem for him throughout the year. He was a bright boy, potentially capable of achieving grade As or above in his GCSEs, but this was in jeopardy because he was constantly being sent out of class or being put on report for annoying and disruptive behaviour. In class he irritated teachers and interrupted their lessons by throwing things at other students and fiddling with anything that came to hand. He rarely managed to remain in class for a whole lesson and his self-esteem was suffering. He was frequently in trouble for blocking or flooding basins or toilets, throwing water at people or jumping in puddles and coming into class with soaking clothes. As Emma had described the emotional tasks of children at each stage of development, this teacher had realised that James's behaviour could be that of a child who may need some support to attend to some of the tasks in the Doing stage. When asked about what was known of his early years, he revealed that James had been adopted as a toddler, an age at which his need to experience the physical environment around him and to explore sensations required sensitive and supportive affirmations from a parent or care-giver. This description helped the head of year to develop a range of activities for James, to run alongside his academic curriculum, which enabled him to indulge his need for Being and Doing. Our team arranged for him to have a regular work placement in a nearby nursery school, where he proved to be responsible and very helpful, attending to the care of children at the sand and water trays. His enjoyment was visible and audible. He would often say to the nursery teacher with a beaming smile 'I'm good at this, aren't I?' Back in his peer-group class, he is given jobs to do, such as testing and operating technical equipment, and is positively encouraged to talk through his observations on experimental activities during science and DT lessons.

James's behaviour in class and around school has settled, and he is now better able to attend to the more serious demands of Year 10 study. The school, in addition, has taken on board that the emotional needs of many of its students –

considered to be young adults – may need to be reconsidered in order to help them achieve the success they deserve and in order for the school to continue to maintain its high level of achievement in the league tables.

4

Keep Taking the TA:
A Letter to Henri Matisse

PATRICIA BLAKE

In order to 'keep taking the TA' I remind myself that Eric Berne opposed professional elitism and the use of complex language; I, like him, want to sit at the 'over-simplified' table with people who are visually creative thinkers and produce games that will help young people understand how TA can help with their relationships and communication with others.

When I feel scared it is normally because my Child has gone to a place in my past and opened a box which has been locked and sealed so securely that you would think even Houdini couldn't get out! When I feel like this, there are two things I usually do. One is to retreat to my bed where it is cosy, warm and safe, and tell myself that it is OK to think and feel at the same time; the other is to write in my dairy to my favourite artist, Henri Matisse. Then the creative daydreamer in me can withdraw, and put my thoughts and feelings into words or pictures. If, on the other hand, I find myself dealing with this feeling from a professional stance, I call on my Parent and tell myself that 'sometimes even the counsellors need counselling', and ask for supervision.

This chapter consists of extracts from my diary, and will explain why I developed the games that I call 'Keep Taking the TA'.

Dear Henri,

During the past five years I have been studying the concepts of transactional analysis and how it can help us to understand our personality, relationships and communication with others.

As part of my work as a behaviour support teacher I work with a wide variety of children and adults who might need guidance, nurturing or structure in their lives. Although TA is not a new phenomenon, to those who have no knowledge or understanding of it, it might seem mind-boggling and complex. As I developed my own understanding I wanted to share my thoughts and feelings with everyone. For example, if TA could help me unlock the boxes of my past and help my Adult to look at things in the here-and-now, then I knew I had a resourceful tool to help others.

Henri, the big kid in me felt so excited, just as I did when I went to an exhibition by Claes Oldenburg, where I was so inspired by his sculptures of 'oversized' everyday objects that I felt myself screaming inside saying 'Quick, go to every school in the country and bring all the children here now'.

TA offers no leaning forks with meatballs and spaghetti, giant fur ice creams or bread-and-butter pudding. Oldenburg says that in his art he is 'concerned with perceptions of reality and composition, which is the only way art can be really useful – by setting an example of how to use the senses' (Oldenburg 1996). I strongly believe that TA, like art, can help us communicate, think and feel in more creative, effective and efficient ways. With this concept in mind the games that I designed were aimed at all age groups from infants through to adult.

Henri, sometimes I ask myself why I became a teacher. It's not that I don't enjoy my job; without a doubt, I do. I tell myself it's because I can empathise with those I meet. With many children I work with, I am reminded of my own past and I have had to keep myself safe by reminding myself that this is not about me and that with my help others can effect a significant change in attitude, thinking and behaviour. Can you remember being at school? I can recall, when I was at school, the teacher would say, 'Sit still, stop fidgeting, get on with your work', or 'Just write down what's in your head'. What she didn't know was that that was the most difficult experience, when there were so many things I wanted to block out, and the Be Strong driver made me hold it all in.

How can a child be expected to conform, or just write down what's in his/her head when all he/she can think of is what is going on in his/her life – the drug or alcohol misuse; domestic violence; sexual, emotional or physical abuse; divorce; adoption; separation from parents; not knowing your parents; being a carer or a refugee; and so much more?

When your self-esteem is low you can't function properly and many of the young people I work with have a self-esteem which is in their boots. That is not to say that they are so disaffected that they need to be in the local EBD school; they may just need someone to talk to or listen to them, and, indeed, help them to understand their behaviour.

In developing my games (Blake 2003) I wanted to use strategies which would help young people with their social skills and emotional development. I chose to use the developmental affirmations (Clarke and Dawson 1998) for finding ways into their world that would be unobtrusive and make them feel at ease. I wanted to develop a resource using TA which would be fun, creative and informative to children's level of knowledge and understanding. I want to tell you about two children who have learned so much from using the games.

THE NURTURE QUILT

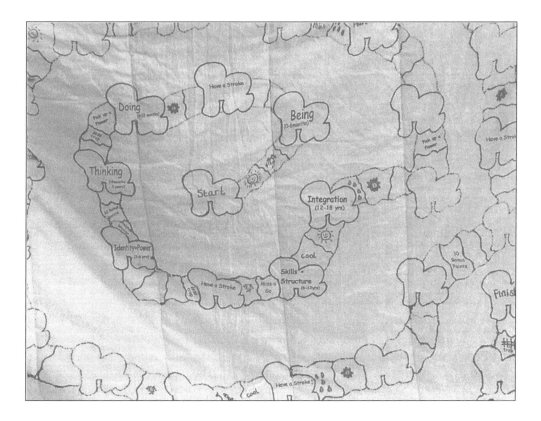

Case study: 'Miss, do we have to do any writing?'

Shaun, a ten-year-old boy, has been separated from his younger siblings and has recently been placed in long-term foster care. Shaun has been a victim of sexual abuse and has witnessed domestic violence. Until recently, he had supervised contact with his parents and siblings, although this arrangement broke down when the parents separated and moved to another part of the country.

The school placed a referral to the BST when Shaun started using sexualised behaviour and language. He found it hard to share resources in the classroom or work collaboratively with others and would become violent towards his peers or teachers, especially females, putting their health and safety at risk.

Following an observation in the classroom and playground it was noted that Shaun was becoming isolated from his peers, he wanted to take control of the group task the teacher had set, and be in charge of the games in the playground, often hitting out in anger when he didn't get his own way, making his peers wary and cautious in his presence.

Following my observations and discussions with the class teacher, we decided it would be a good idea for Shaun to work in a small group with his peers and build on his social skills, work on his anger management and improve his relationships with others.

When I first met Shaun I explained that we would be working together to help him with his behaviour and in making friends. His first response to me was, 'Miss, do we have to do any writing? I don't like writing and I'm no good at maths.' I told him that he didn't need to do any writing if he didn't want to.

Over the following weeks Shaun and I met weekly. We spent time just talking together, and each week Shaun would choose an affirmation that he wanted to hear that day, such as 'All of your feelings are OK here'. He was beginning to feel less angry and safer at school among his peers and adults in positions of authority. In response to 'We want you to be here and want to care for you', Shaun told me that his foster parents were kind, helpful and pleased to look after him, which made him feel happy.

Together, we made a feelings flower tree. He drew a tree and stuck the affirmations on. Or, using my 'Affirmations Baby' poster, which was displayed in the classroom, he would choose an affirmation. After selecting a friendship group, who were mainly the young people he was having problems with, I introduced the Nurture Quilt to the group to help them to develop their sharing skills and relationships with each other. Prior to this I showed the group a set of pictures revealing different emotions and asked them to choose an affirmation for each. Working together as a group they chose, for the 'angry' face, 'It's OK for you to be angry and we won't let you hurt yourself or others'; for the 'happy' face, 'We like you for yourself'; and for the 'lonely' face, 'What you need is important to us'.

In using the quilt the group responded really well, enjoying the softness and cosiness of its feel, they asked if they could take off their shoes and lie on it; they helped each other in taking turns, gave each other affirmations and were further able to discuss the importance of being able to communicate and share their feelings with each other. This was achieved throughout the game; when players landed on a 'contract' they needed to draw one up for themselves from any given scenario, i.e. conflict in the playground, disrupting learning in the classroom. If they landed on a 'trap' the other players would help each other out by saying 'Wait until I get near there and I'll help you', or by making suggestions for helping each other out from their own, real experiences. Shaun found the images used on the quilt of 'The Soul Bird' particularly useful, along with the book of the same name by Michal Snunit (1998). He was 'able to open up the chosen drawer' and discuss things which were concerning him, such as being separated from his family, the anger he felt inside and ways forward for dealing with those feelings.

Shaun is still living with his foster parents and is making good progress at school. In evidence of his improved relationships with others he recently played a leading part in the school play.

I now use the quilt in lots of my social skills groups with pupils of all ages. I have also used it in the youth centres and play centres where I work on a part-time basis.

THE BOARD GAME

In many of the social skills groups I work with, young people find it difficult to listen, share or take turns. While many of them enjoy playing different games, the board game has become very popular. This game enables young people to receive information in a non-challenging way according to age, level and understanding. The object of the game is for each of the players to collect a full cycle while giving and receiving affirmations along the way.

Case study: 'Chloe'

Chloe, a Year 4 pupil, was having difficulty concentrating in class. A pupil with ADHD, taking prescribed medication to help her, the school was finding her difficult to manage, especially in the mornings when she arrived at school, where she would have difficulty separating from her mother, often using the tactic of refusing to take her medication. Chloe found literacy and numeracy difficult and was functioning well below her expected level of development. Chloe's home life was also difficult. Her parents had separated and her mother was living with a new partner whom Chloe did not get on with. Mum had recently had a new baby, and there was an elder brother who she was often violent towards. Chloe particularly enjoyed art and playing and making games, although she would often sulk when she didn't win. I decided to work with Chloe one-to-one to build up her self-esteem and gradually move towards working in a small group. Chloe liked to be in charge and take control of situations, rather than wait to be asked, often butting in on others' conversations in order to get individual attention from the teacher or classroom assistant, or, in games, trying to take over. Using the board game with Chloe seemed an ideal way to help with her concentration skills and for her to receive the affirmations she needed.

First we used the affirmation cards, which have flowers on the back and which are laminated and made to the same size as playing cards. We played a variety of games, such as snap and trumps, to help familiarise Chloe with the affirmations and to help with her reading skills. Each time she would choose one to keep with her for the day. We then played the 'Keep Taking the TA' game as a pair, in which I was able to explain the rules and affirmations to Chloe. We then played the game in the group, where I allowed Chloe to take the lead and explain the game to the group. Within this group Chloe was able to concentrate, share, give and receive affirmations. She was also able to accept that there wouldn't necessarily be a winner, as the rules state that if you have not collected a full cycle you have to revisit and go back to the beginning! Chloe was also able to learn and accept that she could not always be the centre of attention at school, and it was further arranged that she would spend some special quality time with just her mother.

Chloe is now making steady progress at school and receives one-to-one support from a teaching assistant, and she regularly attends out-of-school activities independent of her mother.

I have found that all ages respond well to using the quilt, board game, poster and cards.

Henri, in the galleries of TA I need the theory and accessibility of Berne, Clarke, Goulding and Levin, but I will always call on you for creative and inspirational comfort.

Thank you,

With love,

Patricia.

5

Have I Got the Right Hat On? Using TA to Deliver High-quality Individual Tuition

ANTHEA HARDING

INTRODUCTION

'I hate you, Anthea!' This is not a statement that people would normally want to hear too often, but it is frequently voiced by the children I work with. The reason it is music to my ears will be revealed.

In my role as an educational therapist I work with children who have been permanently excluded from school or frequently excluded on a fixed-term basis for two to three days. Trying as these situations are for the adults involved, I hold to my belief that through their behaviour these children are letting us know what is happening in their lives and are alerting us when all is not well. The child is coping with his/her life in the best way possible and if he/she could be doing things differently he/she would. Throughout my work I endeavour to maintain an 'I'm OK, You're OK' perspective. I affirm the work the school is carrying out in supporting the child and the child's best efforts in being at school. While I often do not meet the parents of the children I work with, I know that they hear about me, and it is important that what they hear is positive. While they face a difficult period in their child's education they need to know and feel that the world is not against them; that they, too, are OK.

While I am working, I have learned to be aware of the egostates and behavioural modes that I am using because I want to encourage co-operation in the children and model appropriate behaviours for them (Barrow *et al.* 2001:13–16). With reference to the work of Mary Cox, I know that I utilise positive behavioural modes from Adult which she describes as 'functioning in age-appropriate and reality-based ways' (Cox 1999), as shown in Figure 5.1.

I have noticed that, to avoid sounding controlling, I use a very gentle tone of voice and say, 'I wonder how it would be if we do X because it might be safer or quicker?' If the child isn't co-operative I then say, still with a gentle voice, 'Well, let's give it a go and see what happens!' This usually works because it is often very different to what they are used to hearing. While we are working I make a point of

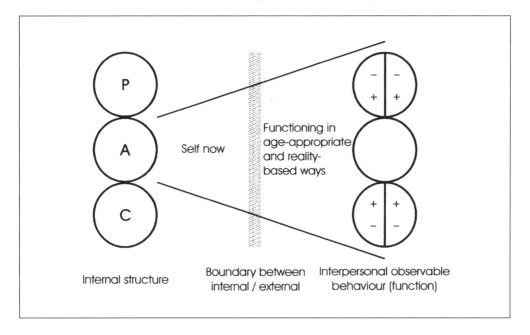

Figure 5.1: Diagrammatic relation of function to structure of egostates (adapted from Cox 1999)

switching to Natural Child, from Adult, and with a hint of laughter in my voice I say, 'Why don't we . . .?' Again, this is not at all what the child is expecting, but it lets them know that learning isn't solely about being serious – you are allowed to have fun.

As I taught for many years I am able to weave some basic literacy and numeracy activities into the sessions I have with children once they know and trust me. Initially it isn't a very popular idea as these children are, generally, underachievers and feel it will be just one more failure, but it is an ideal opportunity to develop their skills and to foster an enthusiasm for learning. Effective education is therapeutic and effective therapy is educational.

GETTING STARTED

When I am invited to a school to meet a child I am often greeted by an adult wringing his/her hands in desperation at the child's latest misdemeanour. That the child can't conform, uses bad language or attacks other children are just three of the complaints I hear, and the adults are running out of ideas as to what to do next. Indeed, for these children, school rules have no relevance, and it is no exaggeration to say that school itself may not make a lot of sense. Often these children have no internal controls and, possibly, no capacity to co-operate. As this is usually the case for most of the pupils I see, I have some idea, before I set foot in the school, as to what I am going to find. In TA language, these children tend not to be accessing their Parent or Adult egostates. What often emerges as I work with the child is that there is a strong message from either one or both parents that they will care for the child's Child if the child will care for the parent's Child, a second-order symbiosis (Stewart and Joines 1987: 202).

On arrival at school my first task is to set up a three-cornered contract between myself, on behalf of the Behaviour Support Team, a member of school staff and the child. I set out how often I will work with the pupil and the type of work I will be carrying out. The school undertakes to provide a suitable room for the work and to allow time for me to meet with the SENCO, the class teacher and the learning support assistant where necessary. With the child I explain who I am, how often I will be working with him or her and the sort of activities and ways in which we will work together.

Our first session is very informal; I ask the child to draw and name the people he or she lives with, and this gives me the opportunity to assess the maturity of his/her work and also check his/her pencil grip. The child's pencil grip may seem such a small detail in the overall picture of the child's behaviour and achievement level, but for some children, learning to hold a pencil correctly and being shown how to form their letters has changed their attitude completely.

Sam, a bright seven-year-old, functioned well above his age group in mathematics, but while his reading was adequate his written English didn't appear to belong to the same child. After asking him to write a few sentences the problem became clear. This boy had no idea of how to form his letters. He always started them at the bottom, so written work was a painful chore. After a few sessions of sitting alongside him Sam now writes quickly and legibly; a whole new world has opened up for him.

Another aspect of seeing the child drawing and writing is that these activities give me a clue as to the child's emerging drivers. From gathering this information it is possible to deduce their potential personality adaptation and see more clearly how to approach the child. Jane's mother frequently addressed her from Controlling Parent, with the result that there was often conflict between them. When I arrived to work with her she would yell, 'I'm not doing it!', even before she knew what I had planned. Her expectation was that I would use Controlling Parent but I approached from Natural Child. Our Child egostates really liked one another and we had many a happy literacy lesson sitting on her top bunk! The majority of the children I work with actually use Controlling Parent in their dealings with others because it is the only way they know of having control over their own world. A further value of the child drawing the people they live with is that it gives me a picture of their initial imago, and what the youngster is imprinting on to school, often with dire consequences (for a detailed account of imago theory see Chapter 6).

Matthew is the youngest of three boys. He is 11 and his brothers are 14 and 16. In our sessions it gradually emerged that he is often bullied by them and to him it seems that no one defends him. Mum experiences poor mental health and it appears that his father rarely engages with his children, as his role is to earn money to keep his family. It is Matthew's dream that Dad will defend him from the bullies, but it never happens and this has become integrated into his own script as an apparent decision to stay a victim. At school he frequently invites other children to hit him but tells them that it is not hard enough and to hit him harder. He then goes to the nearest adult crying, saying that one of the others has hurt him. This is a daily occurrence which the adults refer to as 'what Matthew always does', and it leaves them feeling powerless as there seems to be no solution. At present, he only attends school for each morning because this script is detrimental to his functioning and impacts on the other members of his class. Therefore his negative script needs to be challenged so that he can move on.

During the first session with a child I also play a game with them. Snakes & Ladders is always a good start as the rules are simple and most children are familiar with the game. It does help to endear me to them (I can't be too bad if I am willing to play games). The value for me is in seeing how well they keep to the rules. This is always a good indicator of levels of maturity, and if you can't manage the rules in a board game then it will be hard to abide by school rules. During subsequent sessions I introduce other games so that children experience different rules for different games, leading us into discussions about why we have rules at school, or for crossing the road, for example. A useful activity is to have the child explain the rules and teach the game to another member of the class. This is helpful on two counts: first, because the child has to use their thinking; and, second, the pupils I work with are often isolated due to their lack of co-operation and poor social skills, so they enjoy the opportunity of having another child to work with.

MOVING ON

By the end of my initial meeting with the child I usually have a fairly comprehensive picture of what I need to be planning for them and I base this work on Pam Levin's Cycle of Development (Levin 1982) and Clarke and Dawson's developmental affirmations (Clarke and Dawson 1998). (A full series of developmental stage information, including tasks and affirmations, is provided in Appendix 1.) I close my eyes and imagine how old I would believe the child to be regardless of their chronological age. For most children it is about two years old. That is, in emotional developmental terms, they are at the Doing stage, either because that stage wasn't completed successfully or because the child hasn't yet learnt to think for himself. The information I have gathered at the first session gives an indication of which may be the case.

If I am in any doubt about which stage the child is in I ask them to paint for me. Those who haven't completed the Doing stage seem to have no knowledge of mixing paints to achieve the colour or shade they require. What they use is what they see, and then I know that there is more work to be done in the Doing stage. If their handwriting or pencil grip is causing problems they probably have difficulties related to the Thinking stage and are frustrated by being unskilled in some tasks. So the school could be faced with one of two dilemmas; the child isn't mature enough for what's happening in their school year group or they are frustrated through lack of skills. They are telling the adults in the only way they know how – through their behaviour. This, in itself, is important information; it informs our knowledge of how things may get done, or not get done, at home; it indicates the initial imago and the child's developing life-script.

Case study: John

John is almost 13, and is bright but quite adrift at school. He is very disruptive and is frequently asked to leave the class despite having considerable one-to-one support. As I have got to know him I have learned that his father believes that if you want a child to do something you 'shout at him and tell him what to do', and this is what John brings to school with him. He doesn't have any internal controls and doesn't know how to co-operate, so he often behaves in an inappropriate manner until the adults do just as his father does. For this child school is a daily frustrating and humiliating experience.

Working with this boy and those like him is challenging as he has strong defence mechanisms that have been in place for a very long time. Playing games with John is difficult because, even when presented with a game he hasn't encountered before, he insists that he knows the rules – a very strong Controlling Parent behaviour.

When we work alone together, and therefore have no audience, he constantly makes loud noises like a three-year-old, gets up from his place and walks around the room. He leaves the room if he feels like it, although he never goes far, searches in cupboards and thinks it is in order to help himself to anything that appeals to him. I have grown to like John immensely and to recognise his good heart, so I decided that in order to really make progress I would invite him to help me with a project. I told him that I was worried about some work I had to do. In fact, I was just plain scared, so if he didn't help me I didn't think that I could succeed. At first he was reluctant, but he soon warmed to the idea – I had invited him into his more positive Nurturing Parent.

I arrived at our next meeting clutching a single bed sheet, some chalk and a permanent marker and began by drawing two figures on the whiteboard as shown in Figure 5.2.

I explained to John that I would like him to reproduce the figures on the sheet and suggested that he do the work in chalk first. He was reluctant but put the sheet on the floor and finally drew the figures in chalk. We stood back and viewed his work. I wondered if the head of one needed to be a little larger and felt quite irritated when he said 'No, they'll do'. (I recognised that my own Be Perfect driver was getting in my way and I knew that I had to put it to one side if John was to make progress.)

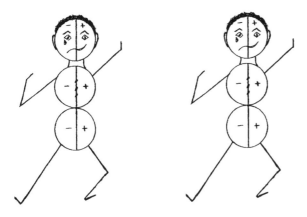

Figure 5.2: Anthea's diagram for John

John worked diligently and we chatted together as he completed the task. Once this was done he stood up to inspect his efforts and said, 'I should have done that one's head bigger!' I assured him that it was a job well done and this proved to be absolutely true. When I have used the sheet with other youngsters there is an appeal in that another child has clearly done the work. What John had done was to draw a picture of him and me. For some reason I am easily identifiable to other children by the red hair, which I do not have!

Figure 5.3: John's drawing

To end the session we stood in each circle and talked about its function and how we transact with others. Rather than refer to PAC, I use Thinking, Doing and Feeling as labels which children easily recognise. The fact that they can actually stand in each circle has also proved to be an immensely powerful tool. John stepped off the sheet and said, 'I don't use my Thinking, do I?'

USING WHAT WE HAVE LEARNT

The sheet with John's drawings is probably my most valuable piece of equipment and I rarely let it out of my sight (see Figure 5.3 above). By the use of a single bed sheet I have been able to give my pupils a way forward, a way of becoming 'unstuck' from behaviours that don't work and discovering new and exciting ways of doing things.

Case study: Matthew

Matthew loves the bed sheet and always checks that I have it with me. He has become extremely skilled at walking through Thinking, Doing and Feeling, and at 'unpicking' what has gone wrong in certain situations. Recently, it has become very clear that his attitude to work is changing and that he is beginning to achieve. He is using his newly discovered Thinking! The last time we met I heard from a member of staff that Matthew had had a bad couple of days; in fact, 'as he used to be'. When I asked Matthew to explain he put the sheet on the floor and stood in negative Feeling. He was hurt that the adults weren't acknowledging his efforts because each time he went to them with stories he had written at home, either the previous evening or before school, they said that they were too busy to look at them. For Matthew, this is a big hurt, and he said that he felt that all his efforts were pointless.

Matthew had become so clear about what he is feeling and thinking, and about what might happen to him if we are unable to find a satisfactory solution to his problem. Together we looked at how he could approach the adults in a way that would get him what he wanted. I suggested that he might say to them, 'I have written this story which I would really like you to read. I know that you're busy now, but if I leave it on your desk would you read it later?' His face lit up! We stood on the sheet and rehearsed the scenario. Matthew got into Thinking, and when he was ready, he moved to Doing and delivered his message. He then went to Feeling and reported on how he felt about that solution. I think 'excited' would describe his reaction. Matthew is learning how to look at situations from a different angle and it is at this point that I would request some time with the teacher to keep him informed and work with him in order to address this child's needs.

Case study: John

When John and I next met we put the bed sheet on the floor and I held up a piece of paper on which I had written 'What do you do when you don't know what to do?' I then gave him the following sum:

$$2 (3 + 4) =$$

to which he replied '14', so I produced the following:

$$a (b + c) =$$

He had no idea what this last sum meant, so I asked him to stand on the sheet in the place where he thought he'd be if he had been given it in class. He went immediately to the negative Feeling place without any hesitation. He said that he would have been so angry that he wouldn't even have listened to the teacher but would have caused a huge fuss and disrupted the class. What he didn't verbalise, and didn't need to, was that the noise he creates regularly in class masks the distress and humiliation he experiences when he can't 'do'. John then surprised me by saying that he was going to make a game for other children. He tore up pieces of paper and put a sum on each one. These pieces of paper he put on the sheet between the two figures and our task was to choose a sum that we could do. He stood in Thinking and made his choice, and I did likewise. We didn't talk about who won; we didn't need to – he was the winner because he had thought about how to keep himself safe. The session ended with John drawing two figures on the white-board; one was me and the other was himself, but he was crying. He drew a red ring around the two of us and said, 'Anthea and John, friends for ever'.

Our next meeting did not start well. John was in and out of the room, so I did what I normally do with any child when the three-year-old behaviour starts – read my book. The inappropriate behaviour stopped very quickly, but as he sat down opposite me I realised that he was crying. He said that he hardly ever cried and couldn't believe that he was doing so. The floodgates then opened and he cried like a baby saying that he couldn't go on. We talked about how difficult each day must be for him and he explained the strategies he uses in the classroom to deflect attention away from his lack of ability. While I felt for this boy, I knew that he had started to use all his egostates. He was allowing feeling to inform his thinking before taking action.

TWO HEADS ARE BETTER THAN ONE

I discovered the power of getting children to co-operate with each other when I was working individually with Tracey, who was referred as a school-refuser, and David, who had been permanently excluded from school. Their paths crossed because often one was leaving our workroom as the other arrived. Each child was curious as to why the other was working with me and what sort of activities I did with them. Although their stories are very different, their curiosity set me thinking about whether or not they could support each other.

Both children were 13. Tracey was still very much recycling the Doing stage and strongly resisted moving into Thinking, so initially she and I worked together in Doing. To move her forward I started taking her swimming or out for a coffee, where she was able to practise her social skills, learn rules and boundaries, and develop her internal controls. When we walked from our workroom to the coffee shop she had to note the route we took because her task was to return us both safely to our base. Once she'd had a 'taster', Tracey then had to earn an outing through co-operating during work periods, although, through all of this, she still refused to go to school.

Meanwhile David had been allocated a place at a new school. We had made a visit and he decided that he really wanted to go. This was a true success story. This very angry boy had arrived in my room stuck with the idea that he was going to return to the school from which he had been excluded because he was 'going to get them' (a negative Rebellious Child response). In fact, he threatened serious damage to those he perceived as having got rid of him from the school and would not be shifted from thoughts and threats of violent behaviour. We worked together on what you do when you're angry, and he was most resistant to any ideas I put forward until I produced an air pump and an inflatable punchbag. That did the trick, and he never looked back.

At the first meeting between Tracey and David we played a board game, and David checked out with Tracey why she was refusing to go to school. He was so excited that he had a new placement and so determined to make a go of it that he couldn't understand Tracey's refusal. This became a recurring theme in their conversations together. When David spoke to Tracey his concern for her was tangible and quite clearly came from Nurturing Parent. During our combined sessions there was a lot of fun and laughter – all three of us in Natural Child – and then came the following event where David addressed all three egostates; a true 'bull's-eye' situation.

I suggested that as the end of term was coming up and we were going to say goodbye to David, the three of us should have an outing. Tracey thought a city farm was a good idea but that we should keep it as a surprise for David. However, as the outing was for him also, I talked to David about the idea of a city farm and he was enthusiastic. Through our joint sessions I had come to understand that, out of his awareness, David had registered Tracey's immaturity, so when I spoke to him about the outing I knew that we both used our Adult and Parent egostates, as illustrated in Figure 5.4.

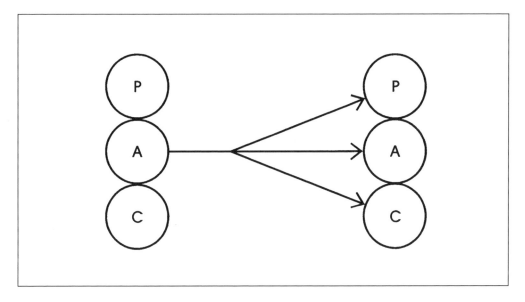

Figure 5.4: Bull's-eye transaction (Woolams and Brown 1978)

We were able to talk about the arrangements, but allowed Tracey to have her excitement. Just before the trip Tracey informed me that she would be bringing a scarf in order to blindfold David all the way to the farm so that it would truly be a surprise for him. I tried talking her out of it, explaining that it could be quite difficult or frightening for David, but Tracey was adamant. At that moment she was really as a three-year-old, so the best I could do for David was to alert him.

The day of the outing arrived and I met Tracey at the support team office before collecting David. As I drove up the road she took body spray, a hairbrush and hairspray from her rucksack in order to prepare for the trip. In her excitement she put body spray in her hair and we were both gasping for air. On arriving at David's house Tracey produced the scarf; but David had used his now well-developed Adult thinking and had brought a bobble hat that he said he would wear over his eyes when we neared the city farm. Fortunately, Tracey agreed to this idea and, true to his word, when I gave the signal David put his hat on, covering his eyes. I have often wondered how we looked to anyone who noticed us! The outing was a great success and each child gave a great deal to the other without realising it. David, indeed, had achieved a bull's-eye transaction (as illustrated in Figure 5.4). He had targeted Tracey's Parent in asking her to take care of herself by not standing behind the horses, and talked to her about things they saw during the day (Adult), and enjoyed holding the chicks and goslings together (Child). Well done, David, you're a star!

FRIENDS INDEED

Tracey had indeed travelled a long road since we had first met, and we began to share some very special moments together. One of her favourite pastimes was to feed the ducks in a local park, so this became a reward that she earned for co-operation in more structured activities. On one particular day, when we had no bread left, we went to the café and decided on ice-cream. We sat outside and I realised that gradually we had leant into one another and were leaning towards each other in companionable silence. When I said it was time to leave, Tracey noticed mud on my shoes that she was worried I would put on the carpet in my car. She offered to go to the café counter and get some tissue in order to clean my shoes. By now I had learned that Tracey could find these tasks difficult – she often lay on the floor in the supermarket if she didn't get what she wanted. But I have learned to catch myself quickly and to look for the positive in situations. I processed how we had enjoyed feeding the ducks together and how we had been sitting in companionable silence enjoying the sun (Child) and how she had used her Nurturing Parent to express concern about the mud on my shoes. I decided to take a chance, we rehearsed what she would need to say in the café, and off she went. I needn't have worried; she returned with a handful of tissues and we cleaned our shoes.

HOW DOES THIS HAT FEEL?

An activity I save for the children until they are really using their thinking is my 'Bag of Hats'. It is just as it suggests – a bag of hats collected from a variety of sources. By now the children have learned about rules in different places, different rules for different situations, the reasons for them being in place and the consequences of breaking them. Now it is time to learn and practise behaving differently in different situations. I invite the child to select a hat that might be their 'home' hat, one that might be their 'school' hat, and so on. I ask them to picture themselves leaving home in the morning, taking off their home hat and putting their school one on. When work begins in the classroom they need to exchange the general school hat for a thinking cap. As we continue our work together I check with the child which hat they are wearing and which one they should have on, so that they learn to change from one situation to another and to behave appropriately. The value of this approach is that, for the child, whatever their circumstances, their home is never criticised: 'I'm OK, they're OK', and their home and family are OK too.

The path the children and I take is often very rocky and uncomfortable for them, but when they are able to use their thinking and feeling to inform their behaviour the outcome is very positive. On our journey together we laugh a good deal, but sometimes these children are very angry with me for challenging their behaviour. When they shout and occasionally throw things, I rejoice because I know that change is taking place. I know that we will soon be friends again and take another step along the road to their success. 'I hate you, Anthea!' is, indeed, music to my ears.

6

Am I In or Out?
Using Imago Theory in
Developing Effective Group Work

EMMA BRADSHAW and GILL WONG

- Why are groups so important to us?
- Why do groups sometimes not work out as we expect?
- How powerful can the image of our initial family group be when taking part in groups?
- How can we use imago theory to help groups grow to become healthy, purposeful and safe?

In this chapter we are going to explore TA theory about how groups develop. We consider the implications of this on group development in schools and use case study material to illustrate this thinking.

INTRODUCING BERNE'S IMAGO THEORY WITHIN BEHAVIOUR SUPPORT WORK

Imago theory was developed by Eric Berne (Berne 1963) and was based on his observations about how groups develop and perform. Berne worked with therapy groups and used his theories to support his clients. In an education context, groups are a part of everyday life and include tutor groups and classes, special educational needs groups and social skills groups, as well as staff-team groups. As part of our work as behaviour support professionals we regularly work with groups who are considered to be functioning ineffectively. Sometimes this may be in the form of whole classes where individual pupils are identified as causing the problem, when actually, the whole class dynamic is problematic. We also come across other groups set up in school to support literacy and numeracy, which have been put together through assessing literacy and numeracy levels and often take no account of the potential dynamic of the groups. Many of the children in the groups have low self-esteem and poor experiences of school. Much of our work involves helping these groups and the individuals in them function in a more co-operative and focused way.

BASIC HUNGERS

From a TA perspective, individuals have three basic hungers: recognition, structure and stimulus. Recognition is a basic human need which, if not satisfied, can result in an acute sense of deprivation. Similarly, we all need ways of structuring time, and being part of a group in various contexts gives us something to do, as well as recognition. We need ways of connecting socially with others and we often seek to do this in familiar ways. Berne maintained that we recreate our ideas about our initial family group and home environment as this feels comfortable – a little like putting on your old slippers. Individuals may do this even if this means recreating ways of getting negative attention. At these times we behave in ways linked to past experience and repeat historic patterns that can be both familiar and unhelpful.

So, let us look at Berne's stages of group development to help us understand how groups function in the context of school.

STAGES OF GROUP DEVELOPMENT

Stage 1: Provisional Imago

At this initial stage, individuals enter a group with a very strong image about what the group is going to be like. This is based on previous experiences of groups the person has had. The dominant image will include recent and longstanding experiences. The family or early care setting tend to have a strong influence on the notion of what a new group might be like. So the first thing that an individual will anticipate is that the group they are entering will be similar to the image of the original family group they hold in their memory. This will include them looking for someone to represent a mother, father and siblings, for example. They will be looking for the leader to be as the leader in their own imago. The leader is a key individual in the early stages of group development. They need to be engaged, attentive and structuring. The problems arise from this stage when an individual's imago, based on historical experience, is significantly different from the group they are entering.

Case study: Jim

Jim is ten years old and he lives with his mother and her partner. He has one older brother who is in secure accommodation. He is hit by his mother's partner and he is often 'put down' and resented by his mother. Recognition and attention in this household tends to be in the form of conflict and put-downs. Jim has been excluded from school. He is often in conflict with teachers, particularly male teachers. He also constantly looks for attention. He does this through getting teachers to shout at him and by becoming confrontational when asked to do things. He annoys other children and does silly things to get them angry. Jim seeks to recreate his home imago in school. He looks for men to get into confrontation with and he expects them not to like him. He looks for women to let him down and believes they are not to be trusted. He looks for peers to be as his siblings and fight with him. He is very effective at generating negative attention. This feels normal for him. Remembering Berne, we all need attention, and negative attention is better than no attention. Individuals need to connect with others – whether positively or, in Jim's case, negatively – to feel alive.

Jim was referred to the Behaviour Support Service and a contract to support his placement was negotiated. A summary of the contract is presented in Figure 6.1.

Jim had problems in his previous school which led to his exclusion. He began a new placement at mid-term, just before Christmas, which was a particularly stressful time in his household due to a lack of money.

Jim's provisional imago (Figure 6.2) has a leader, who is his mother's partner, who is controlling and critical. The partner is violent and abusive and is frequently in conflict with Jim. Jim needs to experience another group that can demonstrate a different way of being. He will need time to get to know his fellow group members, and some pre-start visits have begun to dispel his myths and fantasies.

A group in which he could be accepted and receive positive strokes took the form of a small group that supported Jim into his

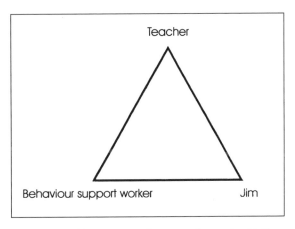

Figure 6.1: Three-cornered contract for work with Jim

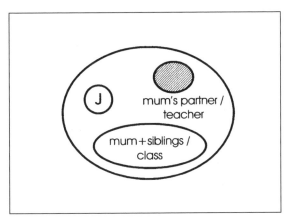

Figure 6.2: Jim's provisional imago

new school. The group had strong leadership from a Behaviour Support Worker who was very present and structuring. The group needed to take part in some structured activities that dispelled any assumptions made by Jim that these people would behave like his family. Getting-to-know-you games were helpful at this stage, including the sharing of safe, non-threatening information, which immediately established people in the group as individuals. He began to see them as separate people and then was much more able to form constructive relationships based on positive, rather than negative, attention. This process alone moved Jim on to the next stage of group development. This provisional stage in group formation is vital as it is the foundation of what will follow. Time spent here is well spent, as this will pay off in later stages in terms of groups functioning effectively.

Top tips for supporting effective provisional stage group development:

- acknowledgement of each key person's provisional imago;
- an established leader is important;
- clear contracting and ground rules are vital;
- safe environments are essential, e.g. a calm classroom where leadership ensures that safe boundaries are in place and put-downs are not acceptable;
- 'why?' questions help to develop thinking and contracting;
- time spent on getting to know each other is time well spent.

Stage 2: Adapted stage

The next stage in Berne's model of group development is the Adapted stage. At this stage the leader is still important but the notion of the group begins to develop as a number of interrelating individuals. This is the stage where setting ground rules and contracting is important. This is when a group may test to see if it is going to be a safe place to be; consequently the rules will be tested by the group to see if they will be maintained. The leader needs to withstand the testing and stay firm and structuring. However, if the leader and the group become unsupportive of each other, and the attention in the group becomes negative, the group process is likely to stay at this stage because, collectively, it will not feel safe enough to develop. Structured and planned activities are helpful at this stage, with the leader very much in control.

Case study: Jim

Jim, at this stage, is in his new class and has established that his small support group are individuals. He sees the rest of the class as two groups of boys and girls. He is testing boundaries at this time to see if they will be enforced. He is also testing to see if the leader will keep him and the class safe. The teacher speaks to Jim in a calm way which Jim responds well to. The teacher also seeks out Jim to give him quiet praise for getting something right. This establishes the rules through positive reinforcement.

Jim is starting to get to know other classmates and to see them as individuals with whom he has had positive experiences working on successful tasks. This helps him feel safe and to realise that it feels better getting positive attention than negative attention (Figure 6.3).

The teacher is still an important figure for Jim, for helping him feel safe in the classroom, but he needs support and help at lunchtimes, when he does not feel so safe. Jim

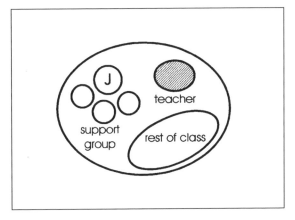

Figure 6.3: Jim's adapted imago

needs leadership and structure here as this unstructured time could easily revert to the old group imago and related behaviours. A Behaviour Support Worker (BSW) works with mid-day supervisors at lunchtimes to structure games and activities aimed at supporting Jim in accessing the social aspects of lunchtime. The BSW also meets with the teacher and Jim to check how things are going and support him by talking things through.

> Top tips for supporting effective adapted stage group development:
>
> - it's OK to test boundaries;
> - time is still needed to develop relationships;
> - unconditional praise and recognition is vital;
> - structured, leader-directed activities are key to completing this stage.

Stage 3: Operative stage

The next stage in Berne's model is the Operative stage. During this stage individuals in the group can fall into familiar patterns to gain attention. This may involve getting into old habits which can often be negative ways of generating recognition. The group joker, the quiet one, the victim, rescuer or bully are all possible roles. The operative stage should not be rushed through or denied, as it is an important part of the group experience, and requires sensitive facilitation by the leader. Given good structure and positive strokes, the time spent playing psychological games – negative, albeit familiar, ways of gaining attention – can be minimised.

The leader needs to encourage the group to work logically on tasks which allow the group to try out different roles. This will help members realise that they can operate in different ways and gain attention in positive ways. They do not have to rely on past negative strategies for getting recognition.

Case study: Jim

Jim is now settling into his new school and class. He knows the names of most of the class and he knows the children whom he relates to (Figure 6.4). Jim is getting into some joking and cussing with a small group of other boys. Sometimes the line between a joke and a put-down is crossed, and he or one of his new friends gets upset and feels excluded from the group. This often happens in unstructured situations. The class teacher monitors this emerging pattern and starts to use the group of boys to carry out specific jobs. They are engaged in a younger year group's football skills sessions as helpers. They are all given a job and clear tasks to do. This gives them opportunities to get positive attention. In class, the boys are separated at times and allowed to work together at others. They are also taught in a small group to understand their emotions and gain self-esteem. The social skills group is run by the BSW and helps pupils make choices about whether to take discounts from each other and about what to do instead.

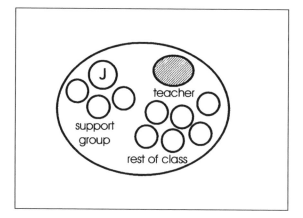

Figure 6.4: Jim's imago operative stage

Top tips for supporting effective operative stage in group development:

- encourage individuals to try out different roles;
- teach emotional literacy;
- keep an eye on the group coming off-task as this could be a clue to them getting into old ways of gaining negative attention;
- leader intervention will re-engage the group positively.

Stage 4: Secondarily Adjusted stage

The next stage in Berne's model is the Secondarily Adjusted stage. At this stage the group start to manage a more intrinsic level of control and begin to support each other. The leader takes on a less prominent role. The group self-regulates its behaviour. The currency of attention is positive and negative attention is not prevalent. The focus of the group is the task they have been set, and they perform at a high level. Individuals embark on risk-taking in their learning and in supporting each other. There is a buzz within the group dynamic and learning is fun for all, including the teacher. The rules and structure are established and there is less need for enforcement.

Case study: Jim

Jim is enjoying being a part of the group and this gives him new experiences to draw on. This is a group which offers Jim a viable substitute for his original family-based imago (Figure 6.5).

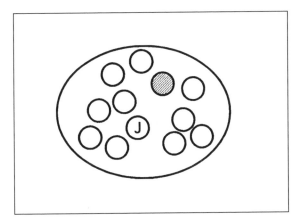

Figure 6.5: Jim's imago secondarily adjusted stage

Top tips for supporting effective secondarily adjusted stage in group development:

- a positive culture within the group will indicate you are at this stage;
- resist the temptation to intervene at this stage; let the group do their own thing;
- be a part of the group and engage in the task with them.

Stage 5: Clarified stage

The final stage in the model is the Clarified stage, when the group focus is on finishing and being able to take and transfer the experience of working in a positive group to other situations. Use of ritual at this stage is vital. Time devoted to finishing the task and for reflecting and reviewing how learning can be transferred to other groups is important. This serves to encourage children in realising that joining a new class, for example in September, could be similar to a successful group experience. In addition, they can contribute constructively to a new group and have a positive experience. (For further details about supporting the closure process see the 'moving on' developmental stage in Appendix 1.)

Case study: Jim

This stage offers Jim a time to acknowledge that it is OK to be sad that things are ending and that saying goodbye is very important. At this stage the mentoring and social skills acquired by Jim in the current safe group are coming to an end. This is done gradually, and reviews of how Jim is feeling about future transition are opportunities to monitor his preparation. There is also the option for Jim to call on support if it is needed, and Jim's confidence is boosted by giving him the responsibility of supporting new Year 7 pupils identified as vulnerable. This project is run by his BSW, and this provides a good way of ending his support gently.

Top tips for supporting effective clarified stage in group development:

- know when to finish;
- review the original contract and check out the original goals and success criteria;
- take time to end and don't avoid closing rituals;
- provide support for finding new roles for group members in future groups – this is as important now as at the beginning;
- affirm that it is OK to be sad.

GROUP IMAGO AND LIFE-SCRIPT

Jim's story supports the optimistic belief that we can change. All of us tend to make assumptions and decisions early on in our lives about how we generate recognition. This can be positive and helpful, or negative and limiting, in terms of personal growth and learning. Our personal ideas about being part of a group contribute greatly to building our individual script which is the story we create about ourselves in the world. We base this story around our earliest experiences; we make the best decisions we can on the information we have available at the time. However, we can also change those initial decisions based on thinking in the 'here and now'. Imago theory can be used as a tool to understand the aspects of group processes we experience, whether they be in the family or at work. We can also use it to enable healthy growth and development in how children learn about themselves and others.

Table 6.1: Summary of group imago stages (based on Napper and Newton 2000)

Provisional	Adapted	Operative	Secondarily adjusted	Clarified
Who's who – find a leader Who will stay? Who will go? This group will be like the last dominant group I have been a part of	Time to find allies within the group Test leader and purpose of the group Some withdrawal – passive/acting out – aggressive	Feel safe Know each member of the group as an individual Express real opinions Act out familiar dramas – ways of getting recognition – group clown/quiet one/serious one	Intimacy Group complete task Support each other Can be family never had! Positive group experience to draw on and transfer	The group ends They take forward their new experiences and apply them to other group situations Mourn the loss; it is OK to be sad and move on to apply learning Knowing when to end or re-start is important
(diagram: leader, me, 'all those others')	*(diagram: leader, other women, me, Kim, Terry, other men)*	*(diagram: closer to leader — Viv the leader, Lee, Keiran, me, Kim, Pat, Terry — further from leader)*	*(diagram: Kim, Lee, Keiran, me, Viv the leader, Pat, Terry)*	
Helping factors • Safe place to meet – room • An established leader is vital • Clear contracting/ground rules • 'Why' questions – why are we here? – what is our purpose? • Location is important • Time to get to know each other – ice breakers/don't try to do task too soon	Helping factors • Testing of rules and boundaries needs to happen so group feel safe • Time needs to be given to people getting to know each other and see each other as individuals – not as 'the sister I always argue with' • Group need to feel safe and lots of unconditional recognition is vital	Helping factors • Identification of unhelpful behaviours – permisssion to do things differently – you can try out different roles • Time needs to be given to exploring different roles • Stage to teach some emotional literacy – I'm OK, you're OK • Everyone can think, everyone can change – good basis for the group to work • Information about process is important – use information to inform decisions	Helping factors • Group fulfilling task • Supporting and encouraging each other • Rules and structure are known	Helping factors • Knowing when to stop • Having good ending rituals

Provisional	Adapted	Operative	Secondarily adjusted	Clarified
Hindering factors • Fluctuating membership – people not there at the start – emotionally not there/passive and withdrawn • Lots of unhealthy assumption by various group members – this is going to be just like the family I have been a part of • No clear function – purpose	Hindering factors • Fluctuating membership can keep a group stuck at this stage • Put-downs – negative strokes can make people feel unsafe and unwilling to share honestly – leading to fantasy	Hindering factors • Group members can stay in unhealthy roles – ways of getting attention and not try out different ways of being – re-enact negative home situations like bullying	Hindering factors • Too much intervention by leader	Hindering factors • Not knowing when to stop/refocus/form • Fizzling out
Stage of development Being/doing	Thinking	Identity	Skills and structure	Recycling

7

It's a Zoo Out There!
Helping Children Cope with Bullying by
Understanding Drivers and Permissions

BEN WYE

- What do young people do when faced with a bully?
- How does TA help us to understand the bully–victim relationship?
- How can we help victims and bullies to act autonomously and with due consideration for others?

In many areas of the country children who are about to leave primary school have the opportunity to experience a range of activities called 'Junior Citizen', which focus on personal safety. Often organised by police officers, events are delivered by a range of trained professionals. The activity described in this chapter was run by behaviour support staff in an inner-London local authority. These transition events are seen as fun and an opportunity to experientially develop personal safety skills and confidence in realistic situations. The event is staged in a variety of locations, from youth clubs to parks. We were lucky enough to use London Zoo for two weeks. Using a controlled public space encouraged in the children a degree of independence while moving between nine different activities. The activity we designed was to allow children to experience, reflect on and develop appropriate responses to bullying.

BACKGROUND

As part of a safety promoting project for children transferring to secondary school, 1,000 children's reactions to bullies were observed. As a behaviour support teacher I was responsible for co-ordinating the exercise and researching the efficacy of the 'Run, Yell and Tell' option developed by Kidscape, a major child protection charity. In preparatory sessions, Year 6 pupils expressed their fear of not coping with bullying at their new secondary schools and of getting into trouble on the way to school. We felt that once the children realised that they could cope with teenage bullies, having faced and 'survived' such a problem, the children would be better able to deal with it in the future. They would have more confidence and would have practised assertive protective skills.

We had experimented with assertiveness training and role play with peers, but we noticed that however good they were in class, children found it a challenge to apply these skills in the real world of the playground. We wanted to allow the children to 'face the fear', and to experience success and confidence when dealing with older aggressive children in as realistic a situation as possible. Therefore, the behaviour support team offered an anti-bullying project as part of the local authority's annual Junior Citizen event for all Year 6 pupils.

In order to assess and improve the pupils' skills in the sort of threatening situations they had identified as being a major worry at secondary school next term, we decided to recreate this 'worst-case scenario' as closely as possible. By ensuring that they experienced success, we hoped that their confidence gained would itself reduce the probability of being bullied. By replacing any ineffective default responses, and providing allower permissions and affirmations, we hoped to develop the assertive skills that would enable them to be more autonomous and effective learners in their new schools.

PROTECTION AND PERMISSION

At the beginning of the activity each class was told that they would be walking between scenarios in small groups and that they would always be in sight of a member of staff, identified by their uniform or badge. The children were also told that they would face various dangerous simulations and should seek adult help if they were worried or concerned.

Permission was obtained through parents and teachers by outlining the nature of the scenario. A contract with the children was made explicit at the beginning of the day. We wanted to release their personal skills so that they might be safer in secondary schools. The staff greeted the groups as they arrived and asked them to wait outside in a quiet public area. When we left the groups we always asked, 'Is it OK to leave you here?' We secured protection by letting the groups know where we were, showing that a police officer was in sight, and told them to call out if they were worried. During this introductory stage we were looking out for any child who seemed nervous. In such cases we would reassure the child that this was only role play and that it was OK for them to watch if they wanted.

We were very conscious of the real threat to the emotional and physical safety of those playing the role of victims. As part of our risk assessment we asked class teachers to notify us of any children who might be vulnerable. We did not put them through the scenario, but got them to observe and join in the practice sessions. A qualified counsellor was on hand to support any child who seemed upset or who wanted to talk about the incident. Out of the 1,000 children involved, only five displayed obvious signs of distress. An important developmental task for children is to separate fantasy and reality, and an awareness of Cycles of Development, and the identity stage in particular, prompted us to ensure that we emphasised that this had been role play, without devaluing their achievements. By introducing the actors and then going through it again, the children enjoyed integrating their thinking and feeling, reflected on their power and identity and learnt new skills. Afterwards we emphasised the unlikelihood of a similar event ever happening, and that none of the adult observers had been involved in a street assault. In the end they were given the affirmation that they could separate acting and real life, and that they had shown that they had not allowed themselves to be victims when, from their perspectives, it had been real.

IMPLEMENTATION

Well before the event we interviewed and trained a dozen 16-year-old drama students from local secondary schools. These were boys and girls, and represented the ethnic diversity of the schools. They learnt a scripted interaction which centred on approaching the younger children in a threatening manner and trying to engage them in teasing banter. The drama students invented more convincing lines, based around the poor quality of their shoes, to mild insults about their schools. These young actors soon became very good at this, adopting a variety of intimidating clothes and walks. One girl, in reality a charming member of a church group, developed a particularly frightening stare, quite as effective as the six-foot police cadet in her group. However, boundaries were clearly set and they always adhered to the 'no swearing and no touching' rules, and were sensitive to children who displayed nervousness. They were taught how to be aware of signs of distress, and, in particular, five responses that they were to look out for in order to feed back to the victims later in the form of colour-coded certificates.

At the zoo we asked each small group of pupils to wait while we went inside the staff marquee. Once we were inside the tent, the 'bullies' sauntered up to the group, looking fairly menacing, and engaged our pupils in conversation, often commenting on the pupils' clothes or asking to see their watches. The bullies carefully increased the tension according to their perception of the resilience of the group until the children showed any sign of stress.

We categorised five indicators of stress using the concept of counter-injunction and driver behaviour (Kahler and Capers 1974) to help us identify the early decisions that children made to ensure they felt OK (see Table 7.1). In other words, that they could remain OK, but only if they were powerful, pleasing, persistent or perfect.

While realising that, up to a point, these were appropriate responses to the bullies, at some stage the responses became unhelpful, for example, when the individual was standing 'frozen' still while the bullies encircled him.

As soon as a response was observed, or up to a maximum of two minutes, the bullies either retreated or staff would emerge from the marquee, where we had been watching, to call the children in, being careful not to appear as if we were rescuing them. While we were congratulating them and identifying what they had done, and also teaching 'Run, Yell and Tell', the actors categorised the children's reactions and prepared to present the appropriate affirmation certificates and re-run the scenario using the taught strategies.

Table 7.1: Summary of responses, drivers, indicators and allowers based on the Junior Citizen bullying scenario

Passive responses to conflict	Drivers 'I'm OK only if I . . .	Early indications noticed by observers and actors	Helpful permissions and allowers given on certificate
FREEZE Do nothing; blank look	**Be strong** 'I never get what I want'	Upright, body defended; still, expressionless, long pauses, short sentences, appears calm. Many children stood with arms folded looking into middle distance, an attitude the police officers advised was not good for personal safety	It's OK to be strong and have needs; be open and say what you want
FLOW Over-adapt; going along with the bully	**Please others** 'I can be OK after this'	Wide eyes, smiles, nods, looks up with head down, palms up, reaching forwards. Voice tone raises at end of sentences; qualifying words, e.g. 'sort of, OK maybe' One child, when asked what type of trainers he had, took them off and offered them to the bully	It's OK to meet your own needs and please yourself
FLAP Panic; confusion	**Try hard** 'Why does this always happen?' 'I almost made it'	Hands to side, cheek or ear. Peers, is tense and gives incomplete sentences; uses words like 'try; difficult; can't think'	It's OK to decide for yourself what to do and to do it
FIGHT or become abusive	**Be perfect** 'I can't be OK until I finish'	Upright, precise; looks to right, mouth pouts; voices in an even steady tone. Tries to provide accurate details. Uses words such as 'exactly' or 'roughly'. Fingers together	It's OK to sometimes give way. You're good enough as you are
FLIGHT Run away or pretend it's not happening	**Hurry up** 'What do I do next?	Agitated; looks at watch; fidgety; screws up face and looks around. Talks quickly, saying 'quick' or 'got to'. Although some children ran as a group to safety, often they were unthinking and would run alone into areas they did not know, putting themselves at potential further risk. We included those behaviours that indicated mental flight, such as the children carrying on talking as if the bullies were not there Life position: – – (This was often combined with another of the drivers)	Take your time. It's OK to think first

Observations

- Many children used variations of the five responses appropriately and maintained their confidence throughout.
- About 5 per cent ran away as soon as they felt scared. Some used raised voices to attract the attention of the nearby adults or to make the bullies back off. One child came very close to pushing the bullies, but he had heard that they were actors, which may have made him feel safe enough to do so.
- Some ignored the bullies so as not to escalate the situation, and then used a different response.
- About 10 per cent kept the bullies talking, some so engagingly that the actors found it very difficult to continue being menacing.
- Drivers keep you going, and, up to a point, the children felt OK. However, when the situation got worse, the pupils' responses became more typical of driver behaviour in order to deal with the perceived reality of the situation.
- Running without thinking was potentially dangerous. One boy broke away from his friends and ran blindly into a cul-de-sac, and could have been isolated by the bullies.
- The most effective flight was by a group of girls from a religious school who stampeded, laughing, through the bullies, while holding hands, and screaming to alert the watching police officers. These children were from a minority religious school where security was always a big issue. In fact, a security guard had accompanied them to the zoo.
- The most striking thing for the adult observers was that of 1,000 Year 6 children, 80 per cent froze. Even when the adults came out and asked the victims if they were OK, sometimes the children would not respond. However, several times the child would show discreet signs, such as mouthing 'They are bullying us' to let us know to intervene. This reflects the national research that 30 per cent of victims had never told anyone in authority about the bullying.

As part of the Junior Citizen programme, each group was scored on a one to five scale to reflect how safe they would have been in a real-life situation. We gave high scores if the group identified a threat and chose to feel, think or behave accordingly to the here-and-now, rather than acting as a script response, while also looking after each other. These were glimpses of the three capacities that Berne associated with autonomy: awareness, spontaneity and intimacy (Berne 1964: 161).

How theory was applied in the learning context

Fear of being attacked can delay learning and is a factor in increasing levels of truancy at the start of secondary school. Nationally, there is a 'dip' in academic performance in the first year of secondary school. Emotional barriers to learning, such as fear of intimidation, are a large factor in underachievement. Travelling alone to school, often for the first time, makes children increasingly nervous. Gangs form as a defence, which can exacerbate the problem.

According to the DfES, bullying happens in all schools (2000/0064). Most definitions of bullying include three aspects:

- that the behaviour is deliberately hurtful;
- bullying is repeated over a period of time; and
- that it is difficult for victims to defend themselves against bullying.

However, young people often describe one-off incidents, such as the role play activity, as bullying.

The approach we used can be compared with other anti-bullying training in that, rather than concentrating on skills, there was also a focus on building self-awareness by reflecting back individuals' responses and existing strategies. In terms of egostates, guidance about what children should do is addressed to their Parent egostate as part of the educational process. By making the scenario 'real' the children were able to experience in the here-and-now an alternative way of making sense of a situation. By reflecting back to them their driver behaviour, the children were able to identify, confront and consider changing, Child egostate thinking.

The fleeting nature of this intervention suggests Berne's notion of the quick cure (Tudor 2002). We felt that the intervention had potency due to its experiential nature, compared with didactic approaches. Compared with class-based teaching, the reality of the scenario means that it was more memorable; all of the 16-year-olds I spoke to remembered the project vividly from their primary school experience. The nine minutes encapsulate the experiential learning cycle (Napper and Newton 2000:1.6), which is presented in Figure 7.1.

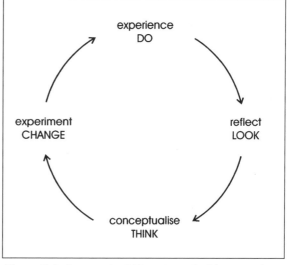

Figure 7.1: An experiential learning cycle (Napper and Newton 2000: 1.6)

JUNIOR CITIZEN AND THE CYCLE OF DEVELOPMENT

The process can also be understood in relation to Clarke and Dawson's (1998) stages of development and affirmations. (For a complete listing of developmental stages and related affirmation see Appendix 1.) The following describes how the role play activity incorporated stages:

Being – The children were excited and apprehensive about going round the zoo alone. The deep fear that this age group still have of becoming lost may have inhibited them from running away from the bullies and meeting the fate met by so many children from the fable of *Hansel and Gretel* to real-life contemporary tragedies.[1] Some had heard about the bullying scenario and were worried. When we greeted them we asked explicitly how they felt, in order to raise awareness. We offered protection by pointing out the adults nearby and told them to call out if they felt scared. We gave affirmations such as 'You can feel all of your feelings', and 'We want you to be here and want to care for you'.

Doing – Participating in the actual scenario. By letting the pupils know they were watched and protected they were offered these affirmations:

- you can explore and experiment and we will support and protect you;
- we like you when you are active and when you are quiet; and
- we like to watch you grow and learn.

Thinking – The children were mobilised from the excitement of the encounter. Immediately afterwards, the children were asked how they felt and to consider other options for dealing with feelings. They were offered a response to the bullies – Run! Tell! Yell! Rather than giving the children 'shoulds' and 'oughts', we presented this as one strategy they *could* try, in different situations. We let them know that we were glad they were thinking for themselves. The actors came in and the children were given the opportunity to ask what it was like in secondary school and what might work in different situations. The observers let the actors lead on this.

Identity – Children clearly had an opportunity to explore what was real and fantasy through the role play.

Skills and structure – Children were encouraged to put new learning into practice by re-enacting the scenario and achieve success. They learnt that they could 'find ways of responding that worked for them' and that they could 'learn from their mistakes'.

The new behaviours were stroked with praise and certificates. These incorporated straight strokes for being OK, thinking and changing. They also included the permission that matched the driver behaviour observed. The text of these is included in Table 7.1. By giving the victims strokes, and allowing the secondary pupil actors to introduce themselves, we also supported an 'I'm OK, You're OK' position, which is associated with assertiveness. A particularly potent stroke was a member of staff announcing a pupil's success loudly to the nearby police officer, known as a carom transaction (Woolams and Brown 1978: 74). It made the stroke public but not intrusive, as it was directed to a third party.

---

1 My chilling warning to stay put, especially in a zoo, was a poem about a boy who was eaten by a lion. James James Morrison Morrison Weatherby George Dupree, who took great care of his mother although he was only three, forgot to '. . . always keep a hold of nurse, for fear of finding something worse'.

PSYCHOLOGICAL RESPONSES TO PRESSURE

Fight and flight are the most familiar survival responses to threat. However, different psycho-social survival decisions are made by infants when they cannot trust that the environment will meet their needs (Clarke 1999: 44–6). The other responses we observed – flow, freeze and flap – may have come about from the nurturing and structuring styles of the children's parent figures.

Clarke and Dawson's Nurture–Structure highway gives a clear picture of how parenting, and teaching styles, can affect personality adaptations to threats (Clarke and Dawson 1998:103).

Tentative care-givers offer less stimulation, recognition and certainty. Their children sense this and learn not to make too many demands on them in case they are overwhelmed. Although this can be supportive, if the strategy fails the child may decide that he must meet his own needs, through creativity or daydreaming. At the extreme end of this continuum, the person lapses into a Walter Mitty fantasy world. One of the children explained her freezing thus: 'I just pretended they [the bullies] weren't there'. Children may well believe that they will only be OK if they can be strong, or if they try hard and please others.

Adults who over-anticipate and impose too rigid a structure, foster children who are dependent on high levels of stimulation. When stimulation is not high, the child will seek it. This may be through using charm or manipulation. In the face of perceived abandonment the child may feel that he or she should be strong or make more effort to please others.

Some inconsistent adults career unpredictably between the extremes of poor boundary setting and rigidity; or between abandonment and over-indulgence. Sometimes a child's behaviour may be greeted with love and sometimes anger. The child learns to be cautious and clever in order to get recognition, but when this fails he/she may become hyper-vigilant and assert his/her own control over self and environment. This may be reflected in the observed freezing, whereby the children were watching and observing before committing themselves to action. This was often to decide to maintain a sense of self-control in the face of the threat – 'I'm OK as long as I stay strong'.

MANAGEMENT IMPLICATIONS FOR APPLYING THE APPROACH

Hyper-vigilant to threat, and in a constant state of anxiety, victims do not make effective learners. As adults we have a responsibility to help victims and bullies to act autonomously and with due consideration for others. First, both victims and bullies need adults to:

- notice and stop bullying;
- empower the victim;
- find and meet the bully's needs.

Most schoolchildren are given clear injunctions about behaviour:

- Don't run;
- Don't shout (Don't say 'no');
- Don't tell tales.

Although these might arguably lead to a well-ordered school, they are not effective as survival skills in relation to responding to bullying. Kidscape recommends the corresponding permissions:

- Run;
- Yell;
- Tell.

School managers may also want to consider the factors that increase the risk of being bullied. These include:

- lacking close friends;
- being shy;
- over-protective family environment;
- being from a different racial or ethnic group to the majority;
- being different in some other obvious way;
- having special educational needs or a disability;
- behaving inappropriately, e.g. intruding or being a nuisance;
- possessing expensive accessories;
- signalling that they would not retaliate; and
- being aggressive or provoking bullying.
  (DfES 2000)

Meanwhile, we can identify seven types of victim:

- **bullied victims** with a history of being bullied;
- **vulnerable victims** are easily identified as being different, and perhaps even threatening to the main group. Children with obvious special needs, or from an ethnic minority are made to feel that they don't belong;
- **passive victims** are ineffectual in the face of attack. These provide an easy target for the beginner bully because they are often smaller, weaker, unco-ordinated and have difficulty making friends;
- **colluding victims** take on the role of victim to gain attention, acceptance or popularity. This can feel comfortable if one is used to being the scapegoat at home and serve a vital role in gratifying others' desire for power;
- **provocative victims**, either intentionally or unwittingly, trigger bullying. One child I know is transferring his rage at his parents onto his classmates; another

feels so unsafe he over-reacts to any perceived sleight and provides a show for the class, and so rewards any bullying behaviour towards him;
- **false victims** can be attention-seeking or suffer generalised anxiety from another source, a point often overlooked by adults;
- **chance victims,** as in our scenario, can be anyone. However, the fear of the meaningless, unexpected, unprovoked attack, against which we have not planned, can be restricting or can affect our demeanour to the extent that we give off signals that invite attack.
(Clarke 2003)

The following permissions might be useful to help these particular types of victims reflect and change how they think, act and behave in relation to others:

bullied victims	It's OK to exist
vulnerable victims	It's OK to be well
passive victims	It's OK to grow up
colluding victims	It's OK to make it
provocative victims	It's OK to be close; it's OK to be a child
false victims	It's OK to be you
chance victims	It's OK to think

Learning to go with the flow

In order to flow in stressful situations, the individual learns how to navigate creatively around the problem, rather than tackling it directly. This requires confidence, awareness and spontaneity. Jean Illsley Clarke identifies 17 ways to flow with a bully (2003). These compare with the strategies used by other experts, such as fogging and partial agreement:

distract

divert

manipulate   re-frame

humour   redefine

befriend   ignore   minimise   maximise

listen selectively

self-talk   act a little crazy

do something unexpected

pre-empt   confuse or derail   join in

CONCLUSION

While this project took place, with the support of 'experts' outside school, what it lacked was the presence of an adult whom the children knew and trusted – someone who was warm and familiar. A class teacher would be best placed to run this type of intervention, and, with careful boundaries, classmates could exchange bully and victim roles. This can create its own problems, but with clear 'de-roleing' it can avoid the risk that realism involves. The key seems to be to give permission to respond to intimidation assertively, according to the circumstance, rather than teach a specific response which some children could find impossible. Responding incongruently could even invite further victimisation. This could be a powerful tool for developing autonomy, something that may be a challenge to teachers and children but which should be the goal of every learning community.

8

Taking the Drama Out of a Crisis: How School Managers Use Game Theory to Promote Autonomy

GILES BARROW

INTRODUCTION

This chapter takes a close look at how school managers have used TA ideas to increase their professional effectiveness in supporting colleagues. The key concepts in this section are the Drama and Winner's Triangles with additional reference to using solution-focused techniques. For the most part, other chapters have considered utilising TA ideas in working directly with children and young people. This chapter is concerned entirely with applying TA ideas to managing staff in the busy context of schools.

A recurring experience for most managers in schools is that of the referred pupil; a familiar story told by dozens of head of years, curriculum leaders, head teachers and deputies. Quietly minding her own business, a head of year is teaching her class. There is a knock on the door and a child arrives. Looking forlorn, the boy has a note in his hand and offers it for scrutiny. 'Damien has been insolent. I will not tolerate this anymore.' After a weary sigh the teacher points the child to a seat and resumes the lesson. A few minutes more and there is another knock, and Sharon enters, simmering with rage, and thrusts a crumpled note on the desk: 'This girl will not settle. I won't have her back until she apologises'. Sharon takes the remaining spare place. Five minutes more and the door opens again, and another émigré gives a familiar grin to his mates at the back of the room and makes do with a chair at the teacher's desk. And so the pattern repeats itself another three or four times during the lesson, with a growing refugee population that is now camped alongside the radiator or standing up in front of the cupboards, passing time with interim tasks.

At the end of lesson the head of year makes a move to discuss matters with the new arrivals but is intercepted by an irate teacher with an accompanying child. Both of them are scowling. The teacher insists on retribution for a misdemeanour and the pupil protests innocence. The head of year now has six pupils lingering from the last lesson, two angry individuals demanding attention and a small queue forming down the corridor comprised of various staff and pupils who all need 'a quick word'. And it's only Monday lunchtime! The task of middle-managing professionals is an unenviable one; high on pressure, low on gratitude and consistently demanding.

KARPMAN'S DRAMA TRIANGLE

What I have been increasingly aware of is the degree to which the experience of middle managers can be understood by using Karpman's Drama Triangle roles, (Karpman 1968). The triangle is shown in Figure 8.1.

In training sessions, participants are especially struck when recognising Persecutor, Victim and Rescuer roles, and the significance of the dramatic switch leading to the game pay-off. On the basis of their experience, middle managers make a range of connections, some of which are presented in Table 8.1.

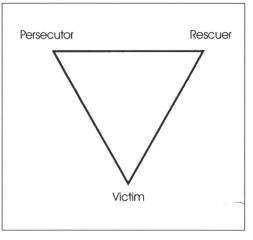

Figure 8.1: Drama Triangle

Table 8.1: Drama Triangle roles and manager's experience

Drama Triangle role	Manager's experience
Rescuer	Feeling obliged to help out other staff struggling with pupils Carrying out discipline on behalf of other staff Negotiating with pupils in the absence of other colleagues Being aware of just how difficult other staff are finding particular classes/pupils Having a sense of being totally responsible for what goes on in year team/curriculum department Being torn between supporting staff and providing respite for pupils suffering poor circumstances
Victim	Feeling utterly exhausted by trying to cope with varied and increasing personal demands Feeling put upon by senior staff who have more time and skills to cope with crises Being at the mercy of the actions of other staff Having a sense of complete chaos with no possibility of change Feeling overwhelmed by the sheer scale of ongoing problems inherent in the role of middle manager; it is an unceasing burden
Persecutor	Becoming fed up with the incompetence/laziness of others Being frustrated with the ambivalent sense of commitment others have for their work A sense that if only others did as they had been told then the situation would not be so difficult A belief that only middle managers really know what goes on in the school; either head teachers are too removed from the classroom or class teachers don't have an idea about the bigger picture

It is important at this stage to emphasise a few features of Karpman's early work on the Drama Triangle:

- Firstly, Karpman maintained that individuals take on game-playing roles out of awareness. In other words, middle managers do not consciously seek to rescue or persecute but that the role emerges when interacting with others. While we don't do this on purpose, game playing can become a familiar way in which people interact with one another.
- Secondly, Karpman noticed that within Drama Triangle situations, individuals create a notion of what happens which negates here-and-now reality checking. In other words, individuals borrow from previous experiences, either from the workplace or elsewhere, and create a perception based on assumptions and partial information.
- Thirdly, Karpman believed that becoming aware of the existence of game playing was a significant step in doing something positive about difficult situations. This chapter considers what we can do, having recognised that games are played in our relationships at school.

Becoming familiar with the roles of Persecutor, Rescuer and Victim can be an important starting point for middle managers reflecting on relationships with staff. Table 8.2 gives some clues about how to recognise game roles.

The most important aspect of the Drama Triangle is the inevitable switch in roles. What we spot in game-playing situations is that individuals who may initially take on a role – for example Rescuer – switch to an alternative as the game is played out. A common experience for middle managers, is that they inadvertently take on a Rescuer role, e.g. by admitting children sent from other classes. This role may be sustained for a lesson, a week or a term. What happens, however, is that the manager switches to Victim role, inundated and overwhelmed by the demands of others, who may now be experienced more as Persecutor rather than Victim.

Switches in roles are important ways of sustaining game playing; individuals generate recognition through oscillating between roles. However, picking up on switches in roles also provides brief opportunities to spot that we are involved in a game. So if you have come out of yet another team meeting with a sense of 'that always seems to happen when I'm in that meeting/with that member of staff/covering that lesson/dealing with that pupil', then you may have succeeded in picking up on a game. This is the first step in doing something about it.

Another way of picking up on game playing is to listen carefully to the language being used by individuals. 'Yes, but . . .', 'always', and 'never' are commonly used in game playing:

'Yes, that's a good idea, but it wouldn't work in this class . . .'
'These kids never behave themselves . . .'
'You always send pupils to me . . .'

Table 8.2: Identifying Drama Triangle roles

Drama Triangle role	Consider
Rescuer Tendency to do things for others Get caught between feeling obliged to help others and balancing competing responsibilities Can do others' thinking for them, i.e. make decisions on their behalf Make assumptions about what others need, i.e. not checking out thinking Life position: I'm OK, You're not OK	Do I find myself doing other people's thinking for them? Do I do tasks for others without checking first if they want me to do them? Do I do things for others which I really don't want to be doing? Do I feel guilty about not doing things for other staff and/or have an experience of divided loyalties at times?
Victim Tendency to feel helpless and hopeless about situations Negates personal potency and focuses solely on emotional experience Preoccupied with what is going – wrong/not possible Life position: I'm not OK, You're OK	Do I feel 'got at' by others? Do others seem to ignore how I am feeling? Do others seem to be making decisions about what I should do without asking me? Do I feel that things just can't get any better – that any progress will be undermined?
Persecutor Tendency to make others do things (for them) Emphasises need for action at expense of others' ideas, thinking and feeling Life position: I'm OK, You're not OK	Do I get frustrated about the incompetence of others? Do I find myself getting my own back on staff by withdrawing support?

If these phrases become typical in conversations between staff, you might consider whether there's a game going on.

MOVING OUT OF THE DRAMA TRIANGLE

Although Karpman's original model provides a memorable and accessible way of understanding game roles, it paints a pessimistic view of how we fail to get along with each other effectively. None of the roles are healthy or sustainable. Consequently, having recognised a game developing, the best strategy is to move out of the game entirely, as opposed to switching to a different role.

There are several ways to move out of a gamey situation, and strategies tend to be based on two principles:

- identifying and responding to what is being discounted by individuals in each role; and
- identifying and responding to the initial good intentions/legitimacy underpinning respective roles.

DISCOUNTING AND THE DRAMA TRIANGLE

There are some general rules of thumb about discounting regarding Drama Triangle roles:

- when **Rescuing**, people tend to discount **others' thinking** and their **own feelings**;
- when **Persecuting** people tend to discount **others' thinking and feelings**; and
- when in **Victim** role, people tend to discount their **own thinking and others' feelings**.

So, in terms of egostates, none of the roles draw on here-and-now Adult egostate thinking, feeling and behaviour. This provides the middle manager with a first clue to what to do to avoid games. Introducing the Adult egostate is a useful starting point for shifting to healthier relationships.

IDENTIFYING GOOD INTENTIONS AND LEGITIMACY

Karpman noticed that, initially, each role was driven by a legitimate purpose:

- The **Persecutor** role was generated by a genuine **need for action**, where something needed to be done – and then became distorted into making people do things and maintaining a highly critical view of others.
- The **Victim** role was generated by a genuine **vulnerability** – and then became associated with a sense of futility and impotency.
- The **Rescuer** role was generated by a genuine sense of **wanting to help others** – and then developed into doing things for others.

By recognising the early good intentions behind each role, middle managers can begin to build another dimension to responding to game playing.

INTRODUCING SOLUTION-FOCUSED BRIEF THERAPY

In developing Adult egostate responses to game playing, middle managers might find it valuable to use solution-focused brief therapy (SFBT) techniques. Although not rooted in traditional TA theory, the approach can be firmly connected to developmental TA. SFBT emerged from the early systemic approaches developed during the 1950s and '60s. Although initially established in the field of family therapy, the techniques have now been incorporated into the fields of social work, mental health, organisations and education. The emphasis throughout SFBT work is on envisioning future solutions, as opposed to rehearsing and refining diagnosis and pathology.

Making the connection between SFBT and developmental TA is straightforward. Take for example three core TA beliefs:

- I'm OK, You're OK;
- everybody can think; and
- anybody can change.

And now consider three key SFBT principles:

- individuals are essentially well-intentioned; they want what is best;
- individuals have experiences of being successful; they are resourceful; and
- individuals can be encouraged to describe their preferred future.

The general emphasis in both approaches is hopeful and accepting, and is typical of other ideas from positive psychology. The challenge for middle managers is in demonstrating these values in responding to problem-focused situations. SFBT techniques provide a highly practical and effective route into making such responses.

SFBT TECHNIQUES AND THE DRAMA TRIANGLE

SFBT techniques are centred on a series of questions that identify the previous success of individuals, articulate what the individual wants, instead of the problem, and encourages others to think about what is going on. Generally, they invite others into Adult thinking while also hooking Child egostate curiosity.

A really important feature of SFBT questions is that they are genuinely open questions; the questioner takes a risk by asking questions to which they really do not know the answer. Instead of asking 'Why don't you get the children to line up before the lesson starts?' (which strongly suggests the teacher ought to do this), we might ask, 'What might happen if the pupils lined up before the lesson . . .?' The task of the middle manager is to avoid doing others' thinking, albeit on a more subtle level, and to ask questions that encourage individuals to do their own. In practice, this means becoming fluent and more expert in managing the discussion than in becoming an expert on a colleague's situation. For managers well-accustomed to taking on the Rescuer role, this might take some practice. A comprehensive listing of SFBT questions and their links with Drama Triangle roles is presented in Table 8.3 opposite.

Table 8.3: SFBT techniques and the Drama Triangle

Solution-Focused Brief Therapy (SFBT) question	SFBT aspect in promoting Winner's Triangle	How SFBT aspect resists Drama Triangle transactions
Tell me about a time when you were really successful	Personal resources	Resists reinforcing Victim role – identifies potency and competency
What has gone well recently?	Personal resources	Resists reinforcing Victim role – identifies potency and competency
How did you manage during that difficult time?	Personal resources	Resists reinforcing Victim role – identifies potency and competency
What is it that you do, or think, that makes you successful?	Personal resources	Encourages shift to potency from Victim
What would be the best-case scenario?	Preferred future	Encourages shift to potency from Victim and resists Rescuer involvement
What would it look like if a miracle happened?	Preferred future	Encourages shift to potency from Victim and resists Rescuer involvement
How have you been managing in this situation?	Personal resources	Resists reinforcing Victim role – identifies potency and competency
What would you see if things improved just a little step?	Next steps	Encourages shift to potency from Victim and resists Rescuer involvement
Can you recall a time when you have been partly successful in a similar situation?	Personal resources	Encourages shift to potency from Victim and resists Rescuer involvement
Tell me the best thing about the situation	Next steps	Encourages reflection and recognition of potency
What are your hopes for the situation?	Preferred future	Encourages shift to potency from Victim and resists Rescuer involvement
What I really pick up on and appreciate is your ability, qualities, expertise, resourcefulness	Personal resources	Accounts for individual and therefore resists reinforcing Rescuer/Victim invitations
How might your abilities, qualities, expertise, resourcefulness be useful in managing this difficult situation?	Next steps	Accounts for individual and therefore resists reinforcing Rescuer/Victim invitations
Is there anything already happening that fits in with what you really want for this situation?	Next steps	Accounts for individual and therefore resists reinforcing Rescuer/Victim invitations

THE WINNER'S TRIANGLE

One way of understanding what goes on when we move from the Drama Triangle is to take a look at Acey Choy's Winner's Triangle (1990). Instead of focusing on individual roles, Choy proposed that any one individual in a game can choose to utilise a combination of qualities in order to resist roles and invite others out of role. The three dimensions of the Winner's Triangle are:

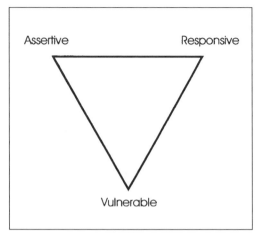

Figure 8.2: Winner's Triangle

- to be **Assertive**;
- to become **Responsive**; and
- to express **Vulnerability**.

Choy maintained that at any time in a game an individual can use the winning qualities to stop a difficult situation. One practical way of doing this is by using SFBT techniques as presented in Table 8.3.

In my work with middle managers I have come across a recurring observation about shifting from a Drama to a Winner's Triangle. Managers often report how useful SFBT questions have been in encouraging staff to take greater responsibility for their situation, recognise their personal expertise and build solutions. Encouraging Adult thinking has been generally useful in changing a difficult relationship with a colleague. Because of this I generally promote SFBT as a first response for managers as a way of creating a winning partnership.

UNDERSTANDING AND RESPONDING TO RESISTANCE

It is worth recalling a crucial observation about Drama Triangle situations; individuals play it at different levels. What we know about game playing is that it is something most of us do, and do on a frequent basis. For the most part it is played at a social level. In other words, individuals find it straightforward to recognise the role they play and how it fits into their relationships with others' roles. At this level we are generally OK about discussing our roles and find it easy to stop game playing. SFBT questions are especially effective in interrupting games played at this level.

We also know that games can be played by individuals at a secondary level which is more deep-seated. For a range of reasons individuals become especially familiar with playing particular roles. It is as if the role has become an integral part of their identity. Consequently, individuals may have a greater investment in maintaining a role; the pay-off is more valuable. In these cases managers may encounter higher levels of resistance to Adult invitations.

In responding to this second-degree level of game playing it can be useful to remind ourselves of what else might be being discounted in addition to thinking. Common situations for middle managers are that not only is the thinking of others being discounted but so also are the manager's feelings (see case study below). An important key in moving forward is for the manager to let others know how they are feeling about the situation without becoming Persecutory. The solution here is for the manager to acknowledge emerging feelings of anger, tiredness and frustration before they overwhelm him/her and are either expressed inappropriately or further suppressed. This can be quite challenging for managers who believe that they must maintain professionalism and remain strong under pressure. It is, however, the critical factor in confronting the game.

Case study: Barry, head of year

Barry is a head of Year 8, a highly experienced teacher and well-established in his school. He is popular with pupils and rarely experiences difficulties with discipline and pupil relationships. Over the course of an autumn term he became increasingly aware of how staff had been sending pupils to him during lessons. Initially, Barry simply incorporated this into his general duties. As the term went on he became irritated by the increasing numbers of children being sent to him. He was also being drawn into resolving break-time disputes even when other staff were on duty. By half-term Barry was exasperated by his situation.

Barry quickly recognised the Drama Triangle situation in a training session. He could spot how he had inadvertently taken on the role of Rescuer in response to the Victim role taken on by teachers in response to children as Persecutors. He also spotted that, over time, he had begun to experience the situation as Victim, and his frustration was fuelling a potential switch for him to Persecutor. Barry also spent time considering how to use SFBT questions and was committed to using them on his return to work.

After a couple of weeks I met Barry again. He was still despondent about the situation. He had found that the SFBT techniques had been helpful for working with several staff who were taking greater responsibility for their classes. He tended to discount this success and focused on the continuing difficulty with two teachers who seemed only to increase their demands as a result of his initial interventions. So we turned to a second strategy. It was time for Barry to take greater account of his increasingly emotional response to the situation. Barry described himself as feeling angry about the teachers' lack of thought for his own weariness and was frustrated about how his lessons were too frequently interrupted by pupils being sent to him. He was also exasperated at how few strategies the staff had implemented, despite his continued support.

Barry talked about his unease in expressing how he felt to the members of staff. He felt it might be unprofessional, and he believed it was his responsibility to remain stoical in the face of adversity. On the other hand, he was seriously worried for his own well-being, and for the first time he had been thinking about looking for a new job. He was also a little worried that he might just snap and tell the members of staff just what he thought of them in decidedly unprofessional terms.

Barry made the decision to assert himself by voicing his vulnerability and asking the teachers to respond to what he had told them. This involved preparing a scripted response to ensure that he minimised the potential of becoming Persecutory. It went something like this:

I have been feeling really angry about what has been going on this term. I am tired of the number of times I have children sent to me and I am frustrated by your not trying out the ideas that I have shared with you over the past two months. I want to know if you have heard what I have said and I'd like to talk some more about this – not now, but maybe tomorrow when we have both had time to think some more about this.

After using this on the next occasion Barry's immediate response was one of relief; that he had, for the first time, been straight about the relationship with the member of staff. He was also relieved that he had not become Persecutor and had encouraged the member of staff to think and given time to do so. It was also important that he referred to needing to be heard – so far that aspect had been denied in the relationship.

In the longer term, Barry's success was due to him finding a way of 'naming the game', a third strategy which is covered below.

NAMING THE GAME AND THE IMPORTANCE OF INFORMATION

Game playing tends to thrive on a lack of information. Bearing in mind the absence of Adult egostate in Drama Triangle situations, providing information can be a highly effective way of reducing game playing. What this means in practice is that middle managers might consider what information other staff currently do not have access to:

- Are they aware of existing protocols for referring pupils out of class?
- Have they been briefed on in-school classroom management techniques?
- Do they know about the school policy on behaviour management, or any recent revisions?

- Have there been recent changes for school managers which have not been passed on to class teachers/tutors?
- Are there any more general contextual factors that staff may not be aware of, e.g. local concerns about specific groups or individual pupils, concerns regarding particular subject areas, imminent local monitoring visits, etc?

There may be information at a more interpersonal level that others may not be aware of:

- Have managers given information about how they are feeling about the situation?
- Has there been discussion about what has been going on in terms of respective responsibilities?
- Are all partners aware of the Drama Triangle roles and game playing?

This last point is worth considering in more detail. Games tend to occur while they remain un-named. In other words, it becomes more difficult to play games and take on roles after they have been explicitly accounted for. It is as if by describing the game playing process and the respective roles it then becomes less satisfying to enter into game playing. If a group of year tutors or a departmental team have been introduced to the Drama Triangle concept, the new information can be used by all parties to resist game invitations and to take greater account of what is really happening. So perhaps the most important step a middle manager can take is to introduce the Drama Triangle to their team.

In training sessions managers sometimes question the wisdom of naming the game. Some believe that it may be too confrontational for staff or too scary a proposition. Others believe their team members will not understand or recognise their part in the game. For these and other reasons managers may withhold information and unwittingly position themselves as Persecutor in relation to their team (holding on to information can be a way in which people establish themselves in a Persecutor role). Other managers have thought about the possible advantages of naming the game which can include the following more helpful responses:

- people might think 'Oh, she's spotted what's going on – we can't play that game anymore';
- people might be relieved that a game has been spotted and engage in finding ways of stopping it;
- people might be intrigued by the idea of the Drama Triangle and want to learn more;
- people might change their ideas about how managers see them in their work.

THE BYSTANDER

The role of Bystander offers a final area for consideration for managers interested in utilising game theory. Petruska Clarkson (1987) offered a significant addition to Karpman's earlier model. Drawn from her experience of living in South Africa during the apartheid era, she proposed that a powerful fourth role is that of Bystander. In this role individuals – or, often, groups – observe the three Drama Triangle roles being played out and watch as individuals switch roles. On the one hand, Clarkson described the Bystander as having a highly uncomfortable experience in that the individual believes they cannot do anything without becoming embroiled in the game. On the other hand, their effective withholding of their involvement impacts on the experience of others and especially amplifies the sense of the Victim's position.

Both staff and children can relate to the discomfort of spectating at another's expense and feeling immobilised for fear of getting caught up in a difficult situation. Incidentally, when introducing the Drama Triangle to pupils, it can be particularly relevant to include the Bystander role where there has been bullying of individuals.

In terms of managing colleagues, it can be worthwhile noting whether game playing is being observed by others. The Bystander discounts their potency and, specifically, their capacity to do something helpful. The antidote for shifting the role to a more healthy position is for the individual to become *involved*. The following case illustrates what this can mean in practice.

Case study: Anne – weak link?

Anne had been identified by her head of department (HoD) as a weak member of the team. Support was arranged with a clear view to helping Anne sharpen up her practice. I was expected to turn this teacher around. The HoD was frustrated at continually covering up for her poor performance (Rescuing shift to Victim) and was determined that something should be done (potential for Persecution). I sensed a high level of annoyance on behalf of the HoD and considerable wariness on Anne's part. However, it became clear, after some initial discussion and observation, that Anne's performance appeared weak when contrasted with the excellent practice of the other members of the department. As a relatively new member of the team Anne was struggling to settle, and found the exemplary work of her colleagues intimidating. What was more important was that there was little communication within the department. Consequently, while there was a sense among other staff that Anne may be having difficulties, only the HoD was fully aware of the disparity between staff performance.

The real weakness for the department was the minimal time given to the team to share successful strategies. Not only was Anne missing out on becoming informed about what worked for colleagues, but also the department was not realising its collective potential. Instead of focusing support on Anne, opportunities were set up for internal departmental discussions about curriculum planning and delivery. In effect, the other subject teachers (Bystanders) had been involved in a way that contributed to greater autonomy for the whole team.

SUMMARY

Staffrooms can offer considerable scope for game playing. Karpman's Drama Triangle is an accessible model for making sense of what can develop in relationships between staff. Middle managers are in a position that is especially prone to invitations to rescue others and, over time, this can lead to limiting relationships for both staff and pupils. There may be several factors that lead individuals into taking on roles, but it is important to remember that, at any stage, people have options to consider, one of which is to stop playing the game.

This chapter has considered how solution-focused brief therapy techniques can provide practical ways of encouraging managers and colleagues to stop the game and take greater responsibility for what happens. I have also presented other strategies that can be used to resist game invitations, including naming the game, involving Bystanders and drawing from the qualities identified in the Winner's Triangle.

Ultimately, the aim is to develop and sustain authentic relationships. Modelling these qualities with colleagues can have significant implications; pupils will be developing their own strategies for managing difficult situations and staff behaviour may provide a useful reference point. Readers can decide for themselves how useful this might be in promoting healthy and sustainable relationships both within and beyond the school gates.

9

3D OK-ness for Schools: Developing Positive School Cultures through Three-dimensional Acceptance

TRUDI NEWTON

'The kids are OK' – and so are the teachers! If we really believe this how do we engage in a process of change? Through an exploration of stories and vignettes this chapter will explore ways of 'walking our talk' by developing principles, attitudes, practical skills and tools that promote the positive philosophy of TA.

The chapter also includes discussion of classroom imagos and related contracts, strokes and discounts, and offers some thoughts and conclusions from the experiences and observations of the contributors to this book in using, and discussing, TA ideas over a number of years.

WHAT IS 3-D OK?

'I'm OK, You're OK' – this is what many people know about TA – and it is a good place to start. In full, and more accurately, it means

> 'I am OK with myself and you are OK with me; I respect and accept myself and you, and trust you to do the same to me.' The subtext of this belief is that when we behave towards those around us 'as if' we and they are 'OK' we invite 'OK-ness' in them. Teasing out the implications of this philosophy we can say that individuals can think for themselves, make decisions, problem solve, grow and change. People may, and often do, behave in 'not-OK' ways; this behaviour is the result of using ineffective strategies for communication and interaction which, with an OK-OK approach and the right information, can be changed. (Barrow *et al.* 2001: 6)

This belief offers us a way of thinking, feeling and behaving, based on the three principles. But schools, like all communities, need another dimension of OK-ness in order to avoid slipping into discounting – 'This school would be great if it wasn't for the kids/teachers/Ofsted/the government', games – 'Look how hard we're

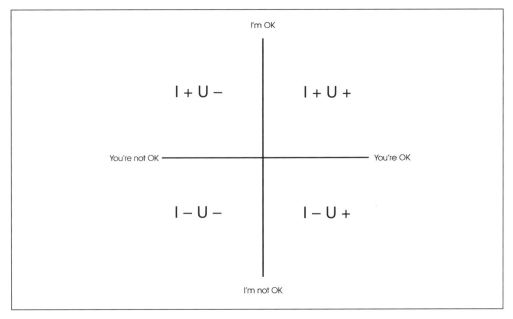

Figure 9.1: Life positions

trying'; 'If it weren't for them'; 'Try and make us'; and negative scripty beliefs – 'There's nothing you can do for some children that will make any difference'.

Berne (1962) originally suggested the polarity of 'I – other' or 'I (we) – You (they)' for positions of OK-ness. Rather than the one-to-one emphasis on I'm OK, you're OK (or not), as shown in Figure 9.1, the real need is for OK-ness with everyone.

A truly I'm OK, you're OK (++) approach is, in fact, to believe, and act as if, I'm OK, you're OK and they're OK (+++). Recently, Chris Davidson (1999) has developed this idea to create a polygonal model of three-dimensional OK-ness, with eight possible positions (Figure 9.2).

When presented to school staff, this diagram is usually met with ironic recognition. Colleagues relate moving around the triangles, as in this example:

Case study

I was standing outside school talking with one of the lads about football (I+U+). As he left, a colleague came up to me and started moaning about this lad and his class. I was soon colluding with him (2) and telling similar stories about this peer group. Then I said that I didn't like talking about the class like that, even if they *were* difficult, and I didn't like him doing either (3). Briefly, I thought 'you are the problem, not the lads' (4) before shifting to a hopeless feeling about the whole school (8).

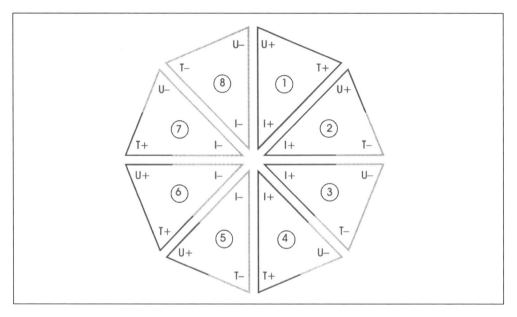

Figure 9.2: Three-dimensional OK-ness (adapted from Davidson 1999)

Sometimes we can hear opportunities to 'start again' in little, everyday happenings. Head teacher Mary Marshall recalls a Year 5 boy who would be well behaved for the first three weeks of each term, then his behaviour would deteriorate to the point where he was regularly sent to her office. When she asked him what happened to make him change he said, 'Well, I start out being good but I never get chosen for anything'.

Every teacher experiences moments like this, realising that children really do know, at some level, what strokes they need in order to learn and thrive. If we listen, and give clear information, we can enable them to voice whatever it is that is a problem. The same is true for teachers.

If we want to change from these familiar scenarios, how might we initiate some 3-D OK-ness in action? One straightforward example from the secondary phase is given in Chapter 2 when Pete Shotton writes about the decision of his team to greet everyone – boys and staff – who they meet in the corridors during the school day.

Another example comes from Nicky Rosewell, head teacher of a middle school that is culturally diverse and has many refugees, asylum seekers and socially dis-advantaged children among its pupils. She tells how during one school year all staff and all pupils were taught PAC, strokes and the Drama Triangle, so that TA became a common language for everyone. This, she says, is not a short-term solution and requires commitment and change from both staff and pupils. She does, however, see evidence of 'TA in action' on many occasions in the school in interactions between children, and between children and adults. The school plans to extend the work to include parents' workshops to 'involve, support and work in partnership with all members of the school community' (Rosewell 2003).

A school which demonstrates 3-D OK-ness in a very tangible way is Mary Seacole primary. Patricia Blake was so enthused by her experience of their whole-school response to Black History Month in 2003 that she began to observe and record what makes this school effective in promoting emotional growth.

Case study

'Sorry you had such a difficult class.'

'They really are hard to manage, can you come back tomorrow?'

'We like having you here the children really appreciate it.'

'That's a school I don't want to go back to.'

'If I clear it with the agency, will you be able to do three days a week?'

For several years I worked as a supply teacher in various London boroughs. At times I would catch myself looking at the clock in the classroom and secretly saying to myself, 'Only another two hours to go and you can get out of here; you don't have to come back; just make sure you get your forms signed and off you go to freedom'.

Tomorrow was always another day, and when I checked in with the agency for the availability of work I could always say no if I chose not to return to a particular school. It wasn't that all the schools I went to were bad, had a demon head teacher or no staffroom or toilet facilities; they just didn't feel right.

So when the agency called at the end of the term and asked what I was doing in September I told them, 'I want to work with children who have special needs, those children who have difficulty managing their behaviour'.

A pattern I had noticed in the schools that I visited was that I would arrive, lesson plans in one hand and resources in the other, and the head teacher would normally say, 'We've split the class up and removed all the naughty ones'. My response was, 'That's a shame, can I have them all back?' It was great, a real challenge, to see if I could manage the whole class, 'warts' and all!

My natural emotions seemed to draw me closer to those pupils who felt disaffected from their class. If only I could spend some time with them, I had a sense that I could help them. At the time, although I was completely unaware of the concepts of TA, I would 'contract' with the pupils around my expectations of their behaviour and their expectations of me for the day or the week. This was normally enough for us to get on with the job of learning and having fun. After all, here I was, the teacher who did things differently. I like listening to music while I study art or eat sweets, and I like playing the latest music during a music lesson, or picking up the chairs and sitting out in the sun when the weather is nice. It's not the creative, free child coming out in me all the time . . . just most of it!

For me, being in one classroom, day in, day out is not my idea of fun. Don't get me wrong, I know it's jolly hard work, but I like fresh air and a variety of environments that inspire and urge me to keep the faith, and spread the love! So when I was offered a job working for the Behaviour Support Team I took the chance of not being based at one school, and, instead, I had the opportunity to experience the diverse cultures, etiquette and techniques of many different schools.

I first discovered Mary Seacole when I took up a full-time position with the team. The school's socio-economic context is poor, with 326 on the roll, and is larger than most primary schools nationally. An opportunity base is attached to the school for pupils aged 5 to 7 with statements of special educational needs. The majority of pupils attend from the local council estate and join the school age 3. One in five pupils is from an ethnic minority group; one in ten is a refugee or asylum seeker, and one in five has English as an additional language. The school has a pupil mobility factor of 26 per cent, with children constantly moving in and out of the school.

When I came to the school with a colleague, as part of my induction, a referral had been sent to the team, as the school wanted help in supporting pupils in the playground. I will always remember my first impressions. In the entrance hall to the reception we were greeted by the office staff, who smiled and directed us to the relevant place. The reception area boasts many pictures and much reference information on the nurse Mary Seacole, after whom the school is named. There are pictures displayed of pupils' work and trophies collected by the various football and netball teams, or the school council. In the staffroom there is always an endless supply of beverages, biscuits, fruit and a photocopier that works! If, like me, you can't remember people's names, the whiteboard always has the day's activities marked, as well as names of visitors to the school and who they are due to see.

Most importantly, there is an air of safeness, comfort and a sense of belonging throughout the school. Teachers or visitors smile at you as you make your way around the school, and pupils often engage you in conversation or ask, 'When are we coming to your group?'

What makes Mary Seacole so different for me? Maybe it's because when I went to the school on my own and met with the head teacher I felt comfortable enough to say 'I'm new and I'm not sure what I'm meant to do!' So together we discussed possible ways forward for the pupils and devised a Partnership Plan that suited everyone – teachers, pupils and timetable. For example, I try not to remove pupils from their lessons unnecessarily. I find that they respond better if they are not taken from their favourite lesson, such as P.E., drama or art. Why do that when you are focusing on their behaviour? At this school you are invited by the pupils to watch them being their best, a great self-esteem boost. This may be in an assembly, a lesson or in the playground.

I know that settling into a new job takes time, I felt I had been given permission to be as creative as I wanted and was immediately made to feel at ease. There's an understanding, like an unwritten contract, that says we can work together as a team, not in isolation or in a broom cupboard. It is more a case of 'what you need is important to us', so much so that if pupils are absent from school the office staff will call ahead and let you know, and if you need resources they will be provided. If there are any events which are taking place, such as a special assembly, sports day or school performance, you get invited so you feel included.

Last year I was invited to open the celebrations for Black History Month, with a whole-school assembly. The pupils listened intensely and participated in my story 'Journey through the Cycle of Development into my Black History'. It tells pupils that they are special, whoever they are, regardless of race, colour, religious belief or socio-economic status. I presented to the school 'a special box' brought back from Jamaica. The box is now situated in the reception area of the school where visitors and pupils are invited to look inside in case they need affirmation. Based on an idea of the head teacher, the box has a mirror at its base and when you look inside you see your own reflection.

With its diverse mix of cultures the school has high expectations of all its pupils. The Ofsted inspection that took place last year reads:

> [this] is a true community school where children are at the centre of education. The behaviour of the pupils and their attitudes to work, their teachers and each other are very positive. The school values all its pupils, seeks their views and acts upon them. The school is held in high regard by the community and is an active part of it.

I thoroughly enjoy working at Mary Seacole and, should I ever feel the urge to go back to full-time classroom teaching, I would definitely apply for a job there. The whole school community like you for who you are; they are open and willing to try new ideas; nothing is seen as impossible. Why? Because at this school the sky's the limit.

Thank you to the staff and pupils who make my working day really special.

FROM PRINCIPLES TO PRACTICE

In order for any group, of whatever size, to work effectively together, there must be a shared value base. Thinking through what 3-D OK-ness means in practice can help to articulate those values. Principles, policies and procedures follow, then practical strategies can be decided. Table 9.1 gives an example from Hills Middle School.

Table 9.1: Values and practice

Philosophy: Intrinsic worth of all people	Value: Respect	**Why** are we doing this? We believe that everyone in the school is important	Example: Realising the need to address behaviour through developing school culture that accounts for all
Principles: Equality, inclusivity	Procedures/policy: Develop behaviour management policy that recognises all	**What** are we doing? Check how our behaviour policy reflects our belief	Example: Promote emotional literacy as a way of changing behaviour management strategy
Practice: Contractual method, positive approach	Action: Implement and monitor new strategies	**How** shall we do it? Change strategies to be more in line with beliefs	Example: Teach TA ideas to all school community

As in fractals, each small part of a school's activity shows the pattern of the whole – and the 'big picture' will be apparent from tiny incidents, like a 'hello', with eye contact and a smile. The reception staff's smile was a tiny fractal for Patricia in her first experience of Mary Seacole, which proved to be the pattern for the whole school. This means that small changes can affect the larger pattern – as in Mary Marshall's recognition of what was missing for one child.

The philosophical, or values, base can be explored further by asking the question 'What is education for?' To some people this may seem a meaningless question – the answer is self-evident. Often those most closely concerned with education – teachers, support staff and parents – are unaware of the differing sets of values on which teaching and learning can be based, and therefore also unaware of the conflict of values that can affect staff, parents and pupils in many subtle ways. Let's take some possible answers to the question:

- Education is a way of passing on our culture and values to the next generation.
- Education is to ensure a supply of qualified workers to fulfil the needs of society.
- Education ensures that all individuals can have the opportunity for self-development and self-actualisation.
- Education is a liberating and empowering process through which people can influence and change their world.

Each of these has merit; however, when one of them is emphasised at the expense of the others it will dictate the contract on which a school operates, at all levels – administrative, professional and psychological. The unconscious conflict this may cause for teachers who are 'out of sympathy' with the prevailing approach will show up as stress and struggle; the effects on pupils may be more devastating. Current focus on the second of the answers above and the consequent emphasis on standards and outcomes sometimes discounts the importance of answer 3 – the humanistic approach – which takes the necessity of appropriate support for emotional development as a prerequisite for effective learning for granted.

Images of learning

Using the imago model we can differentiate approaches to education which result in different 'pictures' of the classroom (Newton 2003).

The first two of the above statements are based on the principle that acquisition of knowledge is at the heart of the learning process. Two more – represented by the third and fourth answers – are person-centred, believing that true learning is relational and developmental.

The liberal classroom

This is a model of education that the majority of us have experienced, and may well form at least part of our introjected Parent and cultural script because of its long history as the archetypal means of teaching and learning. It is the 'traditional' pattern of the classroom, with a teacher whose implied contract with the pupils is 'I tell you; you learn from me', as if learners were empty vessels to be filled by pouring in 'learning'. The focus is on knowledge as information, so cognitive ability, reason and intellectual skills are stroked, while other kinds of intelligences (see, for instance, Gardner 1993) and other learning styles may be discounted. Figure 9.3 shows the imago of this classroom, with the learners undifferentiated.

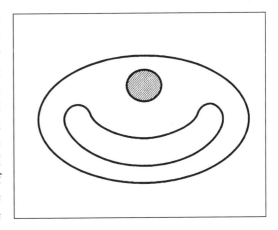

Figure 9.3: Liberal classroom imago

As a traditional method of teaching, with its roots in a belief in the benefits of intellectual development, it has often been used creatively to inspire and kindle a love of learning. However, what many people take on is an expectation that the teacher has all the power and all the responsibility.

The technological classroom

Developed from this 'knowledge' focus, the technological model uses thinking from behaviourist psychology to see learners as material to be shaped by learning. Standards and outcomes are key words, as are rewards and sanctions. The aim is to establish and attain criteria rather than to promote learning as an adventure. The result may be that adaptation and compliance get stroked while creativity and 'open-ended' learning are discounted. The contract between teacher and pupil is ambiguous because the teacher is both instructor and assessor of everyone. The imago (Figure 9.4) shows the teacher in this individual relationship to each pupil.

These two models form powerful 'images of learning'. Of course, what they are saying is important, but if they are not mediated by some aspects of the other two models many children will not be 'accounted for'.

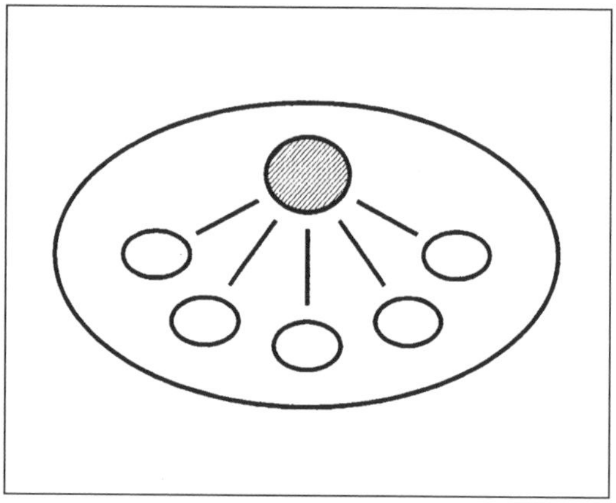

Figure 9.4: Technological classroom imago

The humanistic classroom

For humanistic education the goal is the development of the whole person, and the teacher–student contract can be expressed as 'I support you in your growth to becoming yourself'. Learners are growing plants, to be nurtured and watered. This means that learning/teaching becomes a relationship, and individual worth and creativity are stroked. The emotional dimension of learning is accounted, and pupils are encouraged to accept and help each other. It can be insufficiently challenging for some learners.

Figure 9.5: Humanistic classroom imago

The imago shows the teacher's attention, and class support, for each individual (Figure 9.5). Linda Hellaby's description of her work with her class, and the children's individual growth and support for each other, demonstrates this model in action.

The radical classroom

The radical model of education derives from the writing of Paulo Freire (1972) and proposes a new relationship of teaching and learning in which everyone participates and new knowledge is created through dialogue. The imago shows no 'teacher', since everyone will be learning together in a mutual process (Figure 9.6). The contract is 'we learn together'.

Learners are seen as initially 'imprisoned' by conventional education and the aim is liberation and empowerment – or real autonomy and interdependence in a TA frame of reference. Three-dimensional OK-ness is at the core – everyone involved is respected as both 'learner' and 'teacher', bringing their own experience and resources. This concept of learning has been very influential in adult education. Freire also saw his ideas as applying to children's learning – education is not neutral and either functions to integrate the younger generation into the present system and to conform to it (Freire calls this 'domestication') or it becomes the 'practice of freedom', the means by which people can 'deal critically and creatively with reality and

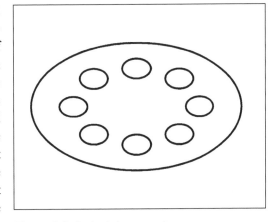

Figure 9.6: Radical classroom imago

discover how to participate in and transform their world' (pp. 13–14). This positive belief in the possibility of change, and in human beings' ability to transform the world (or change the script) is something that this model of education shares with TA – and, in particular, with some emerging perspectives.

A CO-CREATIVE FUTURE

One recent development in TA is the co-creative approach, based on the principles of 'we-ness', shared responsibility and present-centred development (Summers and Tudor 2000). In Chapter 2, Pete Shotton refers to the principles of constructivism as relevant to changing the cultural script. In education, as in therapy, meaning evolves through dialogue, and learning can be the co-creation of new narratives that provide new possibilities. Egostates, transactions and scripts are all co-created through our experience of interaction with others. We can choose to create our new (personal and community) narratives together and we can choose what stories we will tell. An example of this process is the story of Nathan in Chapter 3 – everyone involved in the nursery had a part in making a very different story out of a desperate situation.

This book tells the story of 'walking our talk' by applying TA in schools; it is also the story of a group of people learning together as a 'community of practice' (Wenger 1998). We came together to 'pursue a shared enterprise' – of using TA in schools and reflecting on the results – and brought together our concerns about the communities we work in, our developing practice and issues of meaning and identity. Like Wenger, we asked ourselves,

> . . . what if we adopted a different perspective, [that of] learning in the context of our lived experience . . . what if we assumed that learning is as much a part of our human nature as eating or sleeping, that it is both life-sustaining and inevitable, and that – given the chance – we are quite

good at it? And what if, in addition, we assumed that learning is, in its essence, a fundamentally social phenomenon, reflecting our social nature as human beings . . .? (p. 3)

Our answer has been evident in the way the group has learned together. There has never been a set programme of topics – these have emerged from the priorities and concerns of one or more members at any particular time. Leadership in the group has moved from one to another as people have brought their resources, insights, enthusiasms and discoveries, and seen all of these grow and change as we explored them together. One result has been that there are no limits – the ethos is one of co-operation, potential and positive support; a very different model of training from 'How are we going to get these boxes ticked?'

A co-creative approach is about telling a new story. Another way of saying that, in TA terms, is to invite a change in the script, whether it is the individual script of a disaffected pupil (or teacher), or the cultural script of a school (or a nation).

We have presented some of our 'new story' in this book. We hope that you will want to join us in telling this story, and adding to it, in new places . . . wherever you happen to be.

10

Conclusion

In this last section we want to pull together key strands that are woven into the preceding chapters and also make explicit our understanding and commitment to 'walking the talk' in terms of TA. There are three final accounts we want to share, drawn from the work by some of the previous contributors. Each story describes an aspect of how TA ideas have impacted on the wider context in which children and adults make sense of their learning community.

WALKING THE TALK – CHANGING SYSTEMS

As part of his role, Ben Wye often has the opportunity to support improving behaviour. Like many similar professionals, Ben can spend a lot of time working directly with individual children. Occasionally, though, the focus of intervention is not so much the children but the adults. Working on the assumption that environment significantly influences individual behaviour, the following case study demonstrates the exponential effect of working with the adults.

Case study

A primary school identified substantial concerns about playground behaviour; lunchtimes were particularly difficult with high levels of detentions and fixed-term exclusions causing concern for the school and the LEA, as well as the pupils. Ben decided to provide training for mid-day supervisors (MDS) and Year 6 classes together, in addition to partnership planning for related activities aimed at improving the quality of the lunchtime breaks. Key to the intervention was a series of core TA ideas including Drama Triangle, strokes and affirmations. The onus was on giving staff and older pupils the confidence and skills to reduce conflict and promote play at break. The impact of the project was assessed in terms both of qualitative and data-related terms. All partners reported a high sense of engagement and satisfaction in work. The data presented a striking picture that endorsed the instincts of the adults and is presented in Figures 10.1 and 10.2 below.

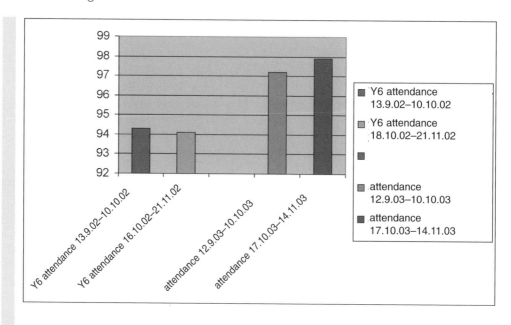

Figure 10.1: Impact of project on attendance

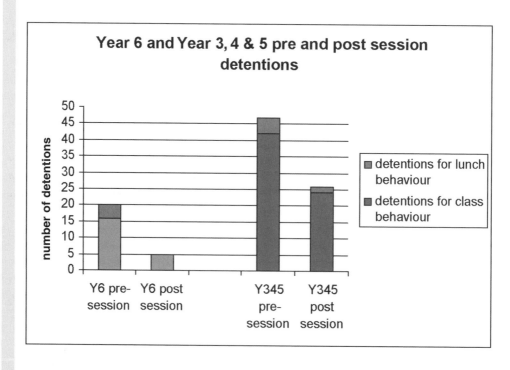

Figure 10.2: Impact of project on number of detentions

To summarise, the impact was as follows:

- For the school as a whole there were 67 detentions in the term prior to the project. This was more than halved to 31 as a result of the input.
- Year 6 total detentions dropped by 75 per cent after the TA sessions, from 20 to five. (Figure 10.2)
- Year 6 lunchtime detentions completely ceased, before the project there were four. For the rest of the year groups the figures went from five to two. (Figure 10.2)
- Year 6 attendance, compared with the previous year, went from 94.2 to 97.5 per cent. (Figure 10.1)
- Comparison of Year 6 attendance the month before and the month after the intervention went from 97.2 to 97.9 per cent. (Figure 10.1)
- The number of days of fixed-term exclusion in the previous corresponding term for Year 6 pupils was six. In the term of the intervention there were none.

An important feature of educational TA is an emphasis on influencing change within the learning context, as opposed to a preoccupation solely with bringing about individual change. Ben's intervention illustrates the importance of multi-level contracting. In other words, while a problem may be presented in terms of student dysfunction, the TA practitioner takes account of potential growth at individual, group and school levels.

WALKING THE TALK: PROFESSIONAL DEVELOPMENT

A second account relates to the work of the Sutton Behaviour Support Service and, in particular, a training event delivered by Emma Bradshaw and Gill Wong. The theme of the training was group work, and Emma and Gill wanted to share imago theory with participants. The process is narrated below and demonstrates how effective professional development is as dependent on managing the training process as it is on content.

Case study

A training event – *Managing Groups* – was offered to a diverse range of individuals from different schools in the borough. The aim was not only to teach participants the imago process but also to take the group through the stages. This course was a new one and, as such, presented a teaching and learning challenge for us. It worked very successfully and was great fun. We wanted to model an effective process of group imago development and here is how we attended to each stage within the day:

Acknowledging the Provisional Imago

- introductions, including asking individuals to find out one thing about the person next to them they didn't already know;
- negotiating a three-cornered contract for the day;
- explanation of Provisional stage;
- task: three pieces of different coloured paper were given to each person and they were asked to write down:
  - who they would like to have dinner with, and what they would like to eat;
  - a favourite book or CD; and
  - a wish for the future.

Each pile of papers was gathered up and shared out so that each person had three pieces of coloured paper. In turns, around the group, each person read out their papers. The participants learnt a little more about the others and identified those who had similar interests and wishes. They also found out some interesting facts about people that may have confronted their first-impression assumptions.

   The group was then split into sub-groups and were asked to think about and record an image of a dysfunctional group they had come across. They were asked to decide which member of their group would draw, role play or write about it, and then replay the scenario to the other groups. The group was then given the opportunity to re-run the situation and invited to take on an unfamiliar role. For example, if the individual would normally tell the story, they might take on an observer role. At this stage a number of participants were prepared to role play, although they said they would not normally have done so.

   During the feedback individuals reported that they could do so because they had got to know each other and they were in smaller sub-groups that felt safe. This activity also served to remind the group why some children with a particular preferred role may need extra support in earlier stages in order to take the risk of trying out a new role or skill.

Developing the Operative stage

In turn, one group stood inside a circle of the whole group. The outer circle threw lots of plastic balls in the air with the inner group given the task of catching as many of them as they could. Each group could have a couple of attempts and use any equipment/props in the room to help them. The balls were all thrown up together. This game is really good fun and involves co-operative communication within the group in order to succeed. Interestingly, there was no mention by the trainers of it being a competition among the groups, but groups set themselves the challenge of trying to beat others.

Moving to Secondarily Adjusted stage

In operative groups participants were asked to write one positive thing about fellow group members. This was completed on hand-shaped cards and everyone in each sub-group gave a positive comment about each member of his/her group. This was after only two hours of contact for most people. It was also noted that this was enjoyed and that no-one expressed any embarrassment.

Arriving at the Clarified Group Imago stage

Conclusion: Let's get the ball rolling

This is a game where the group members stand in a circle and roll a ball to each other, naming an action they are going to take as a result of the course. As each member tells the group what they would do – for example, 'I'm going to get the ball rolling by . . . establishing clearer contracts between class teacher and SENCO' – they place their hand in the circle. All participated and were keen to try out activities on their groups of children.

By the end of the training morning we realised that we had achieved what we had intended – the event had demonstrated the concept of group imago in addition to providing practical guidance on implementation. We had succeeded in taking the group from provisional through to the clarified stage.

The group training exercise serves as an important reminder to TA practitioners that the learning *process* is fundamental to effective intervention. While we may be increasingly aware of this in working with pupils, it is also vital to attend to the process when we invite teachers and others to gain insights into practice. As Trudi Newton has discussed in her chapter, the experiential, collegial approach demonstrated in the above case study underpinned the making of this book, and is key to developing a radical approach to learning.

WALKING THE TALK: MAINSTREAMING TA

Our final story relates a most recent development in which children are increasingly learning about TA ideas within mainstream lessons. Piloted at Grange Middle School in Harrow, and now being used in schools across the country, *The TA Toolkit: Scheme of Work* provides practitioners with a readily prepared curriculum for teaching TA to children. Centred on core TA concepts – including strokes, egostates, transactions, games theory, life positions, rackets and affirmations – the scheme of work has been used with classes of 30 pupils as part of their regular timetable, or as part of group work with pupils targeted for additional support.

To date, feedback from children and professionals has been highly positive; the materials give plenty of permission to schools to take TA into the classroom and directly into the learning process. For teachers recently trained in TA the scheme provides a basis for confident application of the ideas. An example of the work completed by children is illustrated in Figure 10.3.

Figure 10.3: Example of children's work

Rather than being presented as an anger management or social skills programme, the approach emphasises the general benefit for children and adults developing skills for learning about each other and the wider world. In the near future it is intended that children's learning in TA will become accredited through a TA Proficiency Award scheme that would further profile the contribution that TA can make to classrooms and schools.

Ultimately, our intention throughout this book has been to raise awareness about the relevance and accessibility of TA ideas for educators and learners alike. Berne remarked that ideas of real value can be accessed by a child age 7; we have taken him at his word and let those ideas loose.

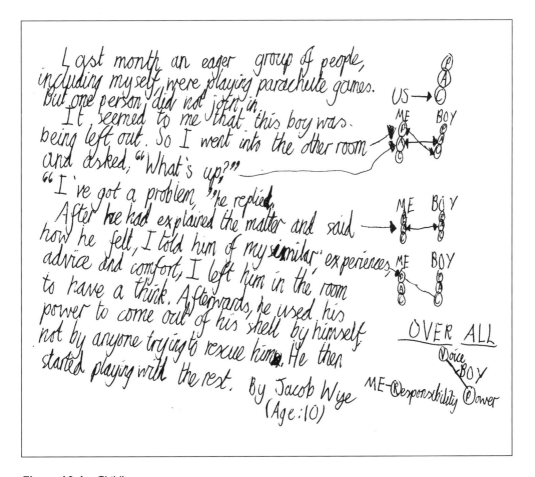

Figure 10.4a: Child's story

I read with a younger boy called Ben just after our lunch break. When I was 7, I learnt about TA and I wondered when it would come in handy. When I was asked to read with Ben, I thought it would be a great opportunity to try it out.

After reading with him one day, I went away and thought about all the strategies I could use.

The strategy I use most is Ego-States. I think about the ego-state Ben is in and the one I'm in and think is this a good situation or not? I am usually in Adult except when Ben is mucking about then I'm in Parent and Adult. I don't think this situation is wrong in anyway because even though I'm being strict, I'm still thinking about the situation.

Using TA has really worked and every body says that Ben has improved, I am very proud of him and myself.

Rosie
Aged 10

Figure 10.4a: Child's story

We have finished with some thoughts from children who have already started walking the talk (Figures 10.4a, 10.4b).

So, when do you take your first step – or your next one?

Appendix 1: Cycles of Development

(Adapted from Jean Illsley Clark and Connie Dawson, *Growing Up Again*, 1998)

Stage One – Being (birth – 6 months)

Job of the child:
- to call for care
- to cry or otherwise signal to get needs met
- to accept touch
- to accept nurture
- to bond emotionally – to learn to trust caring adults and self
- to decide to live, to be

Affirmations:
- I'm glad you are here
- You belong here
- What you need is important to us
- We are glad you are you
- You can grow at your own pace
- You can feel all of your feelings
- We want you to be here and want to care for you

Helpful teacher/carer behaviours:
- Affirm the child in doing the developmental tasks for this stage
- Provide consistent care as needed
- Think for the child when required, while monitoring development through the stage
- Use touch – holding, talking, singing – and intuition to decide how and when
- Be reliable and trustworthy
- Get help if you are unsure how to respond to the child

Stage Two – Doing (6 –18 months)

Job of the child:
- to explore and experience the environment
- to develop sensory awareness by using all senses
- to signal needs: to trust others and self
- to continue to form secure attachments with parents and/or carers
- to get help in times of distress
- to start to learn that there are options and that not all problems are easily solved
- to develop initiative
- to continue Being stage tasks

Affirmations:
- You can explore and experiment and we will support and protect you
- You can do things as many times as you need to
- You can use all of your senses when you explore
- You can know what you know
- You can be interested in everything
- We like you when you are active and when you are quiet
- We like to watch you grow and learn

Helpful teacher/carer behaviours:
- Affirm the child in doing developmental tasks for this stage
- Provide a safe environment and protection from harm
- Provide nurturing touch and encouragement
- Say 'yes' more than 'no'
- Offer a variety of sensory experiences
- Listen to the child, especially if s/he is

struggling to express something
- Feed back observations of behaviour and model new language
- Respond when child initiates activity

Stage Three – Thinking (18 months–3 years)
Job of the child:
- to establish ability to think for self
- to test reality; to push against boundaries and other people
- to learn to think and solve problems with cause-and-effect thinking
- to start to follow simple safety commands – stop, come here, stay here, go there
- to express anger and other feelings
- to separate from parents without losing security
- to start to give up beliefs about being the centre of the universe
- to continue earlier tasks

Affirmations
- I'm glad you are starting to think for yourself
- You can say 'no' and push the limits as much as you need to
- It's OK for you to be angry, and we won't let you hurt yourself or others
- You can learn to think for yourself, and others can too
- You can think and feel at the same time
- You can know what you need and ask for help
- You can be yourself and we will still care for you

Helpful teacher/carer behaviours
- Affirm the child in doing developmental tasks for this stage
- Help transition from one activity to another
- Give simple, clear directions, including basic safety commands
- Be consistent in setting limits and ensuring they are kept
- Accept all of the child's feelings without getting into win–lose battles
- Give reasons, and provide information to move child on in his/her own thinking
- Stroke thinking by encouragement and celebration
- Expect the child to think about his own

and others' feelings
- Give time for new thinking to develop e.g. cause-and-effect

Stage Four – Identity and Power (3–6 years)
Job of the child:
- to assert an identity separate from others
- to acquire information about the world, self, body and gender role
- to discover effect on others and place in groups
- to learn to exert power to affect relationships
- to practise socially appropriate behaviour
- to separate fantasy from reality
- to learn extent of personal power
- to continue learning earlier tasks

Affirmations:
- You can explore who you are and find out about others
- You can try out different ways of being powerful
- All of your feelings are OK here
- You can learn the results of your behaviour
- You can be powerful and ask for help at the same time
- You can learn what is pretend and what is real

Helpful teacher/carer behaviours:
- Affirm the child in doing developmental tasks for this stage
- Expect the child to express feelings and to connect feeling and thinking
- Teach clearly that it is OK to be who you are, and that both sexes and all cultures are OK
- Answer questions accurately, provide information and correct misinformation
- Be clear about who is responsible for what in the classroom and playground
- Encourage fantasy while being clear about what is fantasy and what is reality
- Acknowledge and respond to appropriate behaviour

Stage Five – Structure (6–12 years)
Job of the child:
- to learn skills, learn from mistakes and decided to be 'good enough'

- to learn to listen in order to collect information and think
- to practise thinking and doing
- to reason about wants and needs
- to check out family/school rules and structures
- to learn the relevancy of rules
- to experience the consequences of breaking rules
- to disagree with others and still be wanted
- to test ideas and values
- to develop internal controls
- to learn what is one's own and others' responsibilities
- to learn when to flee, to flow and when to stand firm
- to develop the capacity to co-operate
- to test abilities against others
- to identify with one's own sex

Affirmations:
- You can think before you say 'yes' or 'no'
- You can learn from your mistakes
- You can trust your intuition to help decide what you want to do
- You can find ways of doing things that work for you
- You can learn the rules that help you live with others
- You can learn when and how to disagree
- You can think for yourself and get help instead of staying in distress
- We still want to be with you when we differ and we can learn together

Helpful teacher/carer behaviours:
- Affirm the child in developmental tasks for this stage
- Teach conflict resolution and problem-solving skills
- Give lots of strokes for learning, thinking and finding own way to do things
- Encourage skills development
- Be encouraging, enthusiastic, reliable and consistent
- Respect the child's opinions and beliefs and allow discussion
- Be clear that mistakes are part of learning
- Challenge negative behaviour and confront discounting
- Encourage participation in rule-making, and be clear about negotiable and non-negotiable rules

Stage Six – Integration (12–19 years)
Job of the adolescent:
- to take steps towards independence
- to achieve a clearer emotional separation from family
- to emerge as a separate independent person with own identity and values
- to be competent and responsible for own needs, feelings and behaviours
- to integrate sexuality into the earlier developmental tasks

Affirmations:
- You can know who you are and learn and practice skills for independence
- You can develop your own interests, relationships and causes
- You can grow in your femaleness or maleness and still need help at times
- You can learn to use old skills in new ways
- We look forward to knowing you as an adult
- We trust you to ask for support when you need it

Helpful teacher/carer behaviours:
- Affirm adolescent for doing developmental tasks
- Continue to offer appropriate support
- Accept adolescent's feelings
- Confront unacceptable behaviour
- Be clear about school's position on drugs etc.
- Encourage growing independence
- Expect thinking, problem-solving and self-determination
- Confront destructive or self-defeating behaviour
- Celebrate emerging adulthood, personal identity etc.
- Negotiate rules and responsibilities

Staying awhile – for students in PRU/special unit or centre
Job of the student:
- to develop an attachment to centre staff
- to be sad about their mainstream loss
- to accept attention, support and care
- to test trustworthiness of centre staff
- to understand the status of their placement
- to identify the work they have to do with

the centre and their next placement
- to ask questions about their new placement

Affirmation for the student from centre staff:
- You can count on us
- We will take care of you and of ourselves
- You can push the limits and we will not let you push us away from you
- We want to support you in learning what you need to know about what has happened
- We like you for who you are
- We want to be part of making things better for you

Helpful teacher/carer behaviours:
- Listening to the student talk about their school experiences
- Have work from their previous school available
- Remember that the needs at the main developmental stages can be more pronounced for centre students
- Remember that the student has two education placements – centre and another school
- Answer questions truthfully
- Provide even, confident care

Moving on – for students in transition
Job of the learner:
- to prepare for leaving
- to make connections with the new placement
- to revise/establish expectations of new placement
- to reflect on, and account for, achievements and progress in current placement
- to acknowledge sadness and loss of valued experience
- to prepare practical arrangements for moving on

Affirmation for the child from staff:
- You can carry on growing after you leave here
- Moving on is a normal part of growing up
- We want to support you in moving on in a way that best helps you

- You can prepare for how you want to leave us
- We want to celebrate what you have learned while you have been here with us
- We will still care about you even after you have left

Helpful tutor/pastoral care behaviours:
- Provide opportunities for learners to celebrate and account for achievement
- Acknowledge times of sadness of the learner
- Reassure the learner that support will be continued by others
- Attend to Induction stage tasks and affirmations
- Encourage the learner to take account of their qualities and experience of previous change

Becoming – for students starting at a new school
Job of the child:
- to become aware of the move to the new school/placement
- to gain familiarity with future key carers and locations
- to experience being separate and connected at the same time
- to take steps to prepare practical arrangements for starting a new placement
- to attend to the tasks for the Moving On stage, where appropriate

Affirmation for the child from staff:
- We are pleased that you are coming here
- Your needs and safety are important to us
- We already have a connection with you
- You can decide how you want to be here
- We like you just as you are
- You can be who you are

Helpful teacher/carer behaviours:
- Reality-check preconceptions about the new arrival(s)
- Avoid prejudicing views of the newcomer by previous negative experience
- Gather helpful material and insights regarding the new arrival(s)
- Begin to reach out to the newcomer

Appendix 2: Worksheets for Chapter 1

Stroke Questionnaire

Put a smiley face ☺ next to the sentence, which you would most like to happen.

I like my friends to:
1.   . . . tell me they are glad to see me.
2.   . . . choose me to play because I am good at games.
3.   . . . not make a fuss of me.
4.   . . . tell me to go away

In the classroom I like the teacher to:
1.   . . . joke with me and smile at me.
2.   . . . ask me to do a job.
3.   . . . leave me alone.
4.   . . . tell me off when it isn't my fault.

I like my mum and dad to:
1.   . . . give me a hug.
2.   . . . tell me they are proud of the way I behave.
3.   . . . tell me when I am doing wrong.
4.   . . . give me a smack.

When I meet people I am pleased when:
1.   . . . they want to be with me.
2.   . . . they tell me I am clever.
3.   . . . they notice me when I am being naughty.
4.   . . . they say unkind things about me.

I am pleased when my family:
1.   . . . gives me a hug or a cuddle.
2.   . . . rewards me for being good.
3.   . . . notices me when I make a fuss.
4.   . . . prefers my brother or sister.

The things I like most about myself are:
1.   . . . I am a likeable person.
2.   . . . I am good at work or games.
3.   . . . I keep doing silly things.
4.   . . . I don't like myself.

Scoring
Mostly 1s – prefers positive unconditional strokes
Mostly 2s – prefers positive conditional strokes
Mostly 3s – prefers negative conditional strokes
Mostly 4s – prefers negative unconditional strokes

Positive strokes are needed in abundance. Negative, conditional strokes can be used CAREFULLY to coach in advance, or to correct mistakes. Negative unconditional strokes should never be given.

WORKSHEET A

Send a stroke to a friend

Dear _____   ☺

                                     Name _____

                                     Class _____

Dear _____   ☺

I would like to give you a stroke. My stroke for you is:

_____   Name _____

_____   Class _____

_____

_____

_____

_____

_____

_____

_____

Love from _____

WORKSHEET B

When I am in different egostates I feel, act and behave as follows:

This egostate is Bossy Parent	This egostate is Caring Parent	This egostate is Adult
This egostate is Rebellious Child	This egostate is Whingey Baby	This egostate is Fun Child

WORKSHEET C

Scenarios for children to act/practise being in a specific egostate

Photocopy these situation cards and use in Sharing Circle. Once the children understand what they are doing they will think of many situations themselves.

Ask the children to play a scene in all of the egostates, the rest of the class to act as observers and to report back when the scene has finished.

> You hear the ice-cream van and you want one. It is nearly your teatime. Ask your mum for an ice-cream from Adapted Child (Whingey Baby).

> There is a very special programme on television that you want to see. It is on late and it is school the next day. Ask your dad if you can watch it. Use Critical Parent (Bossy Parent).

> A stranger is talking to you and trying to get you into his car. Act from Rebellious Child.

> It is the holidays. Go to your friend's house and ask him/her to play/act from Natural Child (Fun Child).

> Your teacher asks you to go and find out if the games field is free. Report to him/her from Adult.

> A little child has fallen over in the playground. Help her from Nurturing Parent (Caring Parent).

WORKSHEET D

Scenarios to enable children to practise problem-solving by shifting egostates, thereby inviting the other person to do so.

You would like some more pocket money. You ask in Adapted Child. Your mum says no. Shift to another egostate and try again. What happens? What did you feel like?

You go to your friend's house and ask him (from Adult) if he would like to come out and play. He says 'No'. He says he wants to play on his computer. Shift to Natural Child. What happens then? How did you feel?

The little child you are looking after keeps going on the road. You talk to her nicely in Nurturing Parent (Caring Parent) but she doesn't take any notice. Which egostate do you think would be most effective for you to use to stop her going on the road? Try it out. Were you right?

You are just about to go out to play when your mum says you have to tidy your bedroom. You answer her in Rebellious Child, saying you want to go out now. What happens next? Try another egostate. See if you are able to go out to play *and* see if your mum is OK about the situation.

You are playing about in class. You are in Natural Child (Fun Child), and the teacher gets cross. Keep on in Fun Child. What happens next? Which egostate do you think you need to be in? Practise it. What happened?

WORKSHEET D

References and Bibliography

Ajmal, Y. and Rees, I. (eds) (2001) *Solutions in Schools*. London: BT Press.

Barrow, G., Bradshaw, E. and Newton, T. (2001) *Improving Behaviour and Raising Self-Esteem in the Classroom: A Practical Guide to Using Transactional Analysis.* London: David Fulton Publishers.

Berne, E. (1961) *Transactional Analysis in Psychotherapy*. New York: Grove Press.

Berne, E. (1962) 'Classification of positions'. *Transactional Analysis Bulletin*, **1**(3), 23.

Berne, E. (1963) *The Structure and Dynamics of Organisations and Groups*. New York: Grove Press.

Berne, E. (1964) *Games People Play*. New York: Grove Press.

Blake, P. (2003) http://olpa_productions

Choy, A. (1990) 'The winner's triangle'. *Transactional Analysis Journal*, **20**(1).

Clarke, J. I. (1999) *Time-In: When Time-out Doesn't Work*. Seattle: Parenting Press.

Clarke, J. I. (2003) *Victims, Bullies and Bystanders*. Oxford: Workshop Notes.

Clarke, J. I. and Dawson, C. (1998) *Growing Up Again*. Minnesota: Hazleden (original work published 1989).

Clarkson, P. (1987) 'The bystander role'. *Transactional Analysis Journal*, **17**(3), 82–7.

Cox, M. (1999) 'The relationship between egostate structure and function: a diagrammatic formulation'. *Transactional Analysis Journal*, **29**(1).

Davidson, C. (1999) 'I'm polygonal OK'. *INTAND*, **7**(1), 6–9.

Department of Education and Employment (1999) *Social Inclusion: Pupil Support*. London: DfEE.

Department for Education and Skills (2000) *Bullying: Don't Suffer in Silence*. London: DfES.

English, F. (1971) 'The substitution factor, rackets and real feelings'. *Transactional Analysis Journal*, **1**(4), 225–30.

English, F. (1972) 'Rackets and real feelings, part II'. *Transactional Analysis Journal*, **2**(1), 23–5.

English, F. (1975) 'The three-cornered contract'. *Transactional Analysis Journal*, **5**(4), 384–5.

Erskine, R. (1988) 'Ego structure, intra-psychic function and defence mechanisms: a commentary on Eric Berne's original theoretical concepts'. *Transactional Analysis Journal*, **18**(1), 15–19.

Freire, P. (1972) *Pedagogy of the Oppressed*. London: Penguin.

Gardner, H. (1993) *Multiple Intelligences*. New York: Basic Books.

Hay, J. (1996) *Transactional Analysis for Trainers*. Watford: Sherwood Publishing.

HMSO (2003) 'Every child matters' (Green Paper). London: HMSO.

Kahler, T. and Capers, H. (1974) 'The miniscript'. *Transactional Analysis Journal*, **4**(1), 26–42.

Karpman, S. (1968) 'Fairy tales and script drama analysis'. *Transactional Analysis Bulletin*, **7**(26), 39–43.

Levin, P. (1982) 'The cycle of development'. *Transactional Analysis Journal*, **12**(2), 129–39.

Napper, R. and Newton, T. (2000) *Tactics*. Ipswich: TA Resources.

Newton, T. (2003) 'Identifying educational philosophy and practice through imagos in transactional analysis training groups'. *Transactional Analysis Journal*, **33**(4).

Newton, T. and Wong, G. (2003) 'A chance to thrive: enabling change in a nursery school'. *Transactional Analysis Journal*, **33**(1).

Oldenburg, C. (1996) Exhibition catalogue. London: Hayward Gallery.

Rhodes, J. and Ajmal, Y. (eds) (1995) *Solution Focused Thinking in Schools*. London: BT Press.

Roberts, D. L. (1975) 'Treatment of cultural scripts'. *Transactional Analysis Journal*, **5**(1), 183–9.

Rosewell, N. (2003) 'I'm OK, my school's OK'. *Emotional Literacy Update*, **2**(5).

Schiff, J. *et al.* (1975) *The Cathexis Reader*. New York: Harper & Row.

Snunit, M. (1998) *The Soul Bird*. London: Robinson.

Steiner, C. (1977) *A Fuzzy Tale*. Torrance, CA: Jalmar Press.

Stewart, I. and Joines, V. (1987) *TA Today*. Nottingham: Lifespace Publishing.

Summers, G. and Tudor, K. (2000) 'Co-creative transactional analysis', *Transactional Analysis Journal*, **30**(1), 23–40.

Temple, S. (1999) 'Functional fluency for educational transactional analysts'. *Transactional Analysis Journal*, **29**(3), 164–74.

Tudor, K. (2002) *A Transactional Analysis Approach to Brief Therapy*. London: Sage.

Ware, P. (1983) 'Personality adaptations'. *Transactional Analysis Journal*, **13**(1), 11–19.

Wenger, E. (1998) *Communities of Practice*. Cambridge: Cambridge University Press.

White, J. D. and White, T. (1975) 'Cultural scripting'. *Transactional Analysis Journal*, **5**(1), 171–82.

Woolams, S. and Brown, T. (1978) *Transactional Analysis*. Ann Arbor, Michigan: Huron Valley Institute Press.

To obtain a full catalogue of TA books in print, and self-esteem materials, contact Kevin Smallwood, Charlton House, Dour Street, Dover, CT16 1ED.

Information about training courses and conferences on TA can be obtained from:

Institute of Developmental Transactional Analysis (IDTA)
This is a professional association for those using TA in educational and organisational settings. It is affiliated to the European Association of Transactional Analysis (EATA), and works in close co-operation with ITA. For more information email: enquiries@instdta.org or visit the website at www.instdta.org

Institute of Transactional Analysis (ITA)
The object of the Institute is to educate the public about the study, theory and practice of TA in the United Kingdom. It is affiliated to the EATA. It maintains an Education Network for those interested in using TA in education at any level. For more information contact the Administrator at: admin@ita.org.uk or visit the website at www.ita.org.uk

The EATA Administrator can be contacted on EATA@ntlworld.com

Index